Dear Pastor:

Every once in a while a book appears with a message that seems inspired by God and written *"for such a time as this"* (Esther 4:14). "Your People Shall Be My People," by Don Finto, is such a book. The Church in America is in great need, and Pastor Don Finto gives us great insight into the move of the Holy Spirit in these last days, as well as encouraging words that will inspire you.

This book will expand the Church's understanding about the times in which we live, motivate us to pray for the peace of Jerusalem, and help us know how to support our Messianic Jewish brothers and sisters. The Messiah is returning soon, and we must be about our Father's true business.

Please read this important and timely book. You will be inspired!

Bill McCartney
Coach Mac

National Office ▪ *P.O. Box 103001* ▪ *Denver* ▪ *CO 80250-3001* ▪ *Phone 303 ▪ 964 ▪ 7600* ▪ *Fax 303 ▪ 433 ▪ 1036*

Controversy surrounds God's plan for Israel. Don Finto presents a biblical and exciting perspective of God's heart toward the Holy Land. In so doing, he gives us a valuable and inspiring resource for winning our Jewish friends to Christ.

FRANCIS FRANGIPANE
PASTOR, RIVER OF LIFE MINISTRIES
CEDAR RAPIDS, IOWA

This is the best bridge-building book written on the subject of Israel, the Jewish people and the Church! Go on a journey with my friend Don Finto and learn how you, too, can receive God's heart for His purposes among the Jewish people.

JIM W. GOLL
COFOUNDER, MINISTRY TO THE NATIONS
AUTHOR OF *EXODUS CRY* AND *KNEELING ON THE PROMISES*
ANTIOCH, TENNESSEE

Don Finto's model of trusted and proven leadership indicates a pathway of wisdom and a servant-heart. It's a joy for me to discover his new book!

JACK W. HAYFORD
CHANCELLOR, THE KING'S COLLEGE AND SEMINARY
VAN NUYS, CALIFORNIA

One cannot read this very timely, truly life-changing book without receiving God's heart for the Jewish people. Every believer needs to read *Your People Shall Be My People*.

CINDY JACOBS
COFOUNDER, GENERALS OF INTERCESSION
COLORADO SPRINGS, COLORADO

Here is a book of passion with good theology. Don Finto is passionate for the fulfillment of the destiny of the Church, which includes being a key instrument for the salvation of Israel. I look forward to seeing great Kingdom gain through the widespread distribution of this book.

DANIEL C. JUSTER
DIRECTOR, TIKKUN INTERNATIONAL
GAITHERSBURG, MARYLAND

The Church has many books on Israel, prophecy and the end times, but few have connected us with the heart of God in such a transforming fashion as this one. *Your People Shall Be My People* is the real deal—a call to love God by loving His chosen ones.

STEPHEN MANSFIELD
SENIOR PASTOR, BELMONT CHURCH
NASHVILLE, TENNESSEE

Until the wall of partition between Jew and Gentile is broken, the Church will not achieve the unity and glory promised in the Scriptures. Don Finto's teaching is foundational to the emergence of "one new man"—Jew and Gentile who are one in the Messiah. *Your People Shall Be My People* is mandatory reading for Christians to understand the next, greatest and last move of God's Spirit on planet Earth.

SID ROTH
PRESIDENT, MESSIANIC VISION
BRUNSWICK, GEORGIA

In the spirit of Ruth, Don Finto has expressed the passion of God for Naomi—the Jewish people rejected yet destined for eternal purposes. In humility and loving identification, Finto has expressed the hearts of Messianic Jews to our beloved non-Jewish brothers around the table of our Lord. Dramatically, Israel has returned from exile. Prophetically, this signals a coming rediscovery of Yeshua (Jesus) as our Messiah. Now is the time for the Jewish-Gentile partnership prophesied in the book of Ruth to be fulfilled. *Your People Shall Be My People* could be your doorway to take part in Israel's final redemption.

EITAN SHISHKOFF
FOUNDING DIRECTOR, TENTS OF MERCY
KIRYAT YAM, ISRAEL

Don Finto is a man of integrity, someone who wisely watches over that which has been entrusted to him. A Gentile by birth, his heart has been turned toward the Jewish people, and here he shares that passion with the mainstream of Christianity. *Your People Shall Be My People* is an excellent introduction to both the man and the depth of his passion. This articulate, instructive work draws from the Scriptures and historical writings to give us a better understanding of Israel and the role of the Jewish people in God's plan.

TOMMY TENNEY
AUTHOR OF *THE GOD CHASERS*
PINEVILLE, LOUISIANA

YOUR PEOPLE
— SHALL ✡ BE —
MY PEOPLE

DON FINTO

Regal

A Division of Gospel Light
Ventura, California, U.S.A.

Published by Regal Books
A Division of Gospel Light
Ventura, California, U.S.A.
Printed in the U.S.A.

Regal Books is a ministry of Gospel Light, an evangelical Christian publisher dedicated to serving the local church. We believe God's vision for Gospel Light is to provide church leaders with biblical, user-friendly materials that will help them evangelize, disciple and minister to children, youth and families.

It is our prayer that this Regal book will help you discover biblical truth for your own life and help you meet the needs of others. May God richly bless you.

For a free catalog of resources from Regal Books/Gospel Light, please call your Christian supplier or contact us at 1-800-4-GOSPEL or www.regalbooks.com.

Cover and Interior Design by Rob Williams
Edited by Anne Severance and Deena Davis

Library of Congress Cataloging-in-Publication Data
Finto, Don, 1930-
    Your people shall be my people / Don Finto.
        p. cm.
    Includes bibliographical references.
    ISBN 0-8307-2653-5 (trade paper)
    1. Jewish Christians. I. Title.

BR158 .F56 2001
289.9—dc21   00-045979

6 7 8 9 10 12 13 14 15 / 09 08 07 06 05 04 03 02

Rights for publishing this book in other languages are contracted by Gospel Literature International (GLINT). GLINT also provides technical help for the adaptation, translation and publishing of Bible study resources and books in scores of languages worldwide. For further information, contact GLINT, P.O. Box 4060, Ontario, CA 91761-1003, U.S.A. You may also send e-mail to Glintint@aol.com, or visit their website at www.glint.org.

CONTENTS

FOREWORD

God has sent a few people into our lives to encourage us, rebuke us, direct us, teach us, and above all, to love us and love us well! Don Finto is at the top of our list.

And from this man, who not only married us and prayed our children into existence but also guided us on two tours of Israel, comes a work that is a celebration of his passions. Don is passionate for the Word, and he is passionate for God's people, both Jew and Gentile. We heartily endorse Don Finto, his vision and his new book!

We pray that it will be used by the Lord to remove the scales from believers' eyes concerning the ongoing role of Israel in God's affairs. God opened our eyes through Don's teaching, and now we pray with new vision for the peace of Jerusalem. We're confident that after reading this book you will, too.

Michael W. and Debbie Smith
Nashville, Tennessee

ACKNOWLEDGMENTS

My life has been greatly enriched through my messianic Jewish brothers and sisters. Thank you, Eitan Shishkoff, for embracing my stumbling Gentile heart as I was learning about Jewish believers. John Dawson and Dan Juster, you will never know how grateful I am for the invitation to join the Toward Jerusalem Council II steering committee, participating with you in calling the Church to repentance for her sins against the Jewish people. Thank you, Marty Waldman, Evan Thomas, David Chernoff, Bob Cohen, David Rudolph and Ilan Zamir (who has already gone to meet the King) for welcoming me on the committee and sharing your lives with me these three years as we have revisited history and repeatedly entered the throne room together.

David Chernoff, it was through the reading of your mother's book that the Lord enlarged my heart to devote much of the remainder of my life to bring about understanding in the Church and continually to challenge my Jewish brothers and sisters to believe it is time for their own relatives to come to faith in the Messiah. Be forever thanked.

Thank you, Dan, David, Eitan, and Asher Intrater for accepting me as an equal partner in Tikkun, the apostolic messianic Jewish governing council with ministry in the United States, the former USSR and Israel as well as other parts of the world.

Without you, Anne Severance, this book would never have happened. It was the Lord who continually brought your name to me when I was praying for an editor. You have believed in me, encouraged me, drawn out the best of me, challenged me and made me look like a good writer.

Bill Greig II and Kyle Duncan, if you had not listened to the passion of my heart, you would never have waded through my first writing attempts to welcome me as a Gospel Light/Regal author. Thank you for loving me and trusting me. And Cal Tarrant, your e-mail inviting me to lunch, letting me know that you, one of my former sheep in Nashville, were now in the marketing department of Gospel Light, was a tremendous blessing. Thanks for trusting that I do have a message whose time has come and for challenging me to participate with you in finding ways to spread it.

I have had many intercessors, some who have been praying for many months that I would be able to get this heart message in print. Betsy Headden has repeatedly called others to pray when she knew I was at a standstill. The Lord has constantly given further revelation and insights. May the Lord bless you, Betsy, along with Ann Bell, Barbie Doyle, Jessica Austin, Beverly Boulware, Pat Gee, John Hooker, Shirley Holland and many, many others.

To Stephen Mansfield and my Belmont Church family, I shall forever be grateful for your encouragement, your love and continued support.

My faithful assistant for many years has a heart as big as the world and a love for Israel and the Jewish people that equals my own. Thank you, Sandra Elkins, for keeping my life in order while I was dreaming about the message of this book.

Can you imagine what it is like for a wife to be married for 48 years to a man who is constantly changing? God knew that you, Martha, could survive and still love and trust me. Thank you for letting me ascend to the computer day after day, night after night, to get this passion reduced to print. Let's take a few days and find a secluded beach or mountain resort where we can catch up on life together.

And once I was almost finished with the writing, I knew that I needed you, David Hooper, along with Carl Kinbar, Dan Juster, Eitan Shishkoff and Avner Boskey to read what I had written to be sure that it was accurate. You were able to see things I would not have noticed, and this brought sharper focus to the whole project. I appreciate this beyond my ability to express it.

To You, O Lord, I shall be forever thankful that You have allowed me to see some of Your purposes in our day and to be one of the instruments for challenging the Church to embrace this revelation. Nothing is more rewarding than to be a participant in Your work. Help me to keep growing, to keep learning and to walk humbly before You, so You can continue to use me in Your eternal plan.

INTRODUCTION

The biblical story of Ruth is much more than the beautiful love story of King David's great-grandparents. Ruth is the symbol of every Gentile who has ever come to faith through Israel's God. The words of this Moabitess to her Jewish mother-in-law, Naomi—"your people shall be my people and your God my God"—are still ringing in the hearts of every non-Jew who believes in Boaz and Ruth's promised Son, Messiah, who would come down through their lineage. Every Gentile believer has come from the land of famine to the spiritual realm of abundance in that Name. Even Jesus' reference to Himself as the Bread of Life hearkens back to this ancient love story—to say nothing of the fact that He was born in the shadow of the very fields where Ruth was gleaning, just outside Beth-Lehem ("House of Bread").

But the Church has not responded to her Boaz as Ruth responded to hers. The Church did not leave her Moabitish ways behind when she came into the house. Although she may have taken the "Bread" of Boaz, which represents Jesus to us, she turned her back on all His relatives, the Jewish people.

This is why I must write. This is why I must add yet another book on Israel to the scores that have already been written. My bookshelves are lined with volumes about this tiny nation, her return from exile and dispersion, the reestablished state, the revival of the Hebrew language and how all of this may relate to end-time prophecy. I also have many books written by or about the growing messianic Jewish population. What could possibly be added?

Some of what I am writing is not new. It is written, perhaps, from a different perspective, but it is not new. That Israel's return to the Land is the fulfillment of prophecy and that it signals the nearness of the Lord's return to the earth are common themes in Christian circles. Even so, some of you who have read widely in this area will be drawn to this book.

For others, the information may be fresh revelation. Recently, I was visiting with a pastor who, though passionately pursuing the Lord and desiring to know His Word, knows nothing of God's purposes for Israel. The prophets have been like closed books for him, telling only the story of what has already been fulfilled. Until recently my friend had never considered reading the Prophets to find events that have not yet come to pass.

He, as I did in earlier years, has taken clear words of Scripture about Israel's future and applied them to the Church or has assigned these rich storehouses of prophetic treasure to the dusty bins of already fulfilled history. After our conversation, this young pastor will begin a fresh reading of biblical prophecy. He wants to know what he has missed! It is for such men and women that I have written this book.

Another pastor friend of mine is not likely to read it. He has already made up his mind that "Jesus of Nazareth was the fulfillment of the Old Covenant and the end of God's preparatory people, the children of Israel," as he wrote to me. He believes that "there is no such thing as a messianic Jewish community" and that "the Kingdom of God is not fulfilled in an apostate people who are descendants by blood instead of by the seed which is only through faith." I love this man and pray that he, too, will reread the prophetic words in both the Old and New Testaments and that God will open his eyes to what I am seeing.

Some of what you will be reading here has been stated by others, but those books have not been widely distributed. I have drawn greatly upon such sources in learning about Israel's priestly role to the nations, the hatred of the established Church toward the Jewish people throughout much of our history, the Jewishness of the Early "Church" and the "gentilizing" of the Church.

You will find some material that may be new to you. I believe the Lord continued to give me moments of revelation even in the writing. For years I have been fascinated by the relationship between the present world revival and the rise of the messianic Jewish believing community. I have never heard anyone make these comparisons, though 400 years ago a few of our Christian leaders were beginning to mention that the return of Jewish people to their homeland and their spiritual awakening would coincide, accompanied by a great world revival.

My experience in the messianic movement has brought me to a clearer understanding of Jewish hearts, an awareness I do not find among many Christian pastors. I am passionate about seeing that my Jewish brothers and sisters are accepted as Jewish and encouraged to express their faith within a Jewish framework. I want to see the Gentile Church appreciating her own Jewish foundation stones. I want her to understand why Israel and the Jewish people are center stage in world history again, and I want her to be grateful for a returning Jewish leadership in the Body of Messiah.

As the Church understands the prophetic times in which we live, we will become better partners with God in hastening the fulfillment. We will confess personally and on behalf of the Church for the centuries of persecution of Jewish people and will become ardent intercessors on their behalf, looking for every opportunity to bless and not curse them.

I have come to see the believers from the nations foreshadowed in Ruth, who was the non-Jewish great-grandmother of King David. Though she did not come from the seed of Judah, she came fully into the heritage of Israel. Unlike the Church, however, Ruth did not bring her Gentile ways with her. She left her own people and covenanted herself to Naomi and later to Boaz. She committed to live and to die with Naomi and her people. I believe that should be the Gentile Church's stand with God's covenant family, whose promises we have now entered.

In order to make this book more accurate in the context of our Jewish roots, I have chosen to use terms that are meaningful to both Jew and Gentile. For example, I will not use the word "church" in reference to congregations of Jewish believers. Jewish assemblies will more often use the word "congregation," [an equally good translation of the Greek *ekklesia*, literally, "the called-out ones"]. In this book you will find "church" capitalized when the meaning is the Gentile Church at large.

Most of the time I will refer to the Messiah rather than to the Christ. That is because I have chosen to use the translation from the Hebrew rather than the Greek. "Christ," for many Jewish people, has become a hated word, since many of the atrocities leveled against them have been perpetrated in that name.

I personally enjoy using Jesus' Hebrew name, Yeshua, because that would be the name by which Miriam (Mary), His Jewish mother, referred to Him. Realizing that this term may seem strange to many readers, I have used these two names almost interchangeably.

Sometimes in my writing I refer to the Jews, but even this name—a derivative of Judah, Israel's dominant tribe in the southern Kingdom and Jesus' own tribe—has taken on negative connotations for the Jewish people. I don't believe I have ever heard a Jewish person introduce himself or herself with the words "I am a Jew." Rather, "I am Jewish." Therefore, in this book I speak of the Jewish people, the sons of Israel, God's covenant people. I love the Jewish people and will do whatever is necessary to make my speech more acceptable to this persecuted, closest blood family of our Lord.

These are some of the thoughts that have motivated me to share my heart. I have never considered myself a writer and yet I believe I am seeing things that have not been written or widely circulated. I invite you to hear me out prayerfully and, like the Bereans mentioned by Luke in Acts 17:11, search the Scriptures to see if I am correct.

Listen to Ruth, our non-Jewish covenant partner, as she speaks to her Jewish mother-in-law: "Wherever you go, I will go; and wherever you lodge, I will lodge; your people shall be my people, and your God, my God" (1:16, *NKJV*).

Could this be the covenant pledge we must make with the Jewish people? If you agree, may your life never be the same! May you become a zealous advocate of Israel and Israel's children, fervently pleading their case before the Father's throne.

THE BEGINNING OF THE END

When these things begin to take place, stand up and lift up your heads, because your redemption is drawing near.

LUKE 21:28

God promised Abraham, "I will make you into a great nation and I will bless you; I will make your name great, and you will be a blessing. I will bless those who bless you, and whoever curses you I will curse; and all peoples on earth will be blessed through you" (Gen. 12:2,3). If this ancient promise is still true, and it is, then no person, no congregation, no nation or people group will ever receive their fullest blessing until they learn to love the Jewish people.

I have not always been so passionate about this truth. Let me tell you why I believe these are prophecy-fulfilling times in which we live and how I, a West Texas farm boy, became involved in the messianic Jewish community and came to love this covenant people.

In the early '50s, my wife, Martha, and I were fresh out of college, newlyweds and ministering in postwar Germany. The nation was disgraced and divided; homes and neighborhoods were emotionally and physically destroyed. We were young and idealistic and wanted to be a part of directing this humbled people back to God.

As a Bible major in a Christian college, I graduated confident of what I believed. I knew how to read the Bible to overlook certain passages and to interpret others so that they always said what I had been taught. We knew that any other understanding of Scripture would separate us from close friends and family. Occasionally this would make me uncomfortable. I would read Scripture that did not quite fit what I had been taught. But after all, my professors, who were godly men, knew better than I. They read Hebrew and Greek, and they could not be wrong.

Then the postcard arrived. I remember it as if it were yesterday.

I hated that card! It embarrassed me. It challenged me. It rattled me. I thought the young man who had sent it, a freshman student at the University of Hamburg, arrogant. I showed the card to no one, not even to Martha. I tore it up and discarded the pieces almost immediately.

And yet I could not forget it. I can still quote it verbatim: *"Lieber Don Finto, liest Du die Bibel, um zu sehen, was die Bibel sagt, oder liest Du sie nur, um eine Predigt vorzubereiten?"* "Dear Don Finto, do you ever read the Bible just to find out what it says, or do you just read it to prepare a sermon?" The card was signed "Helmut."

I read the Bible regularly, but I knew at the core of my being that I often studied the Bible to defend positions already held rather than studying to see if these positions were biblically accurate. Did I really want to know God's heart on every issue? Would I be willing to change my belief even if it meant estrangement from those who were closest to me? I desired that of others. What about myself? For the next several years, Helmut's card held me accountable and was a constant reminder to ask the Lord for understanding.

After eight years in Germany, Martha and I returned to the United States, where I began teaching German and some Bible courses in a Christian college. The Charismatic Movement was sweeping the nation and many people were rethinking long-held beliefs. This was also the beginning of the hippie years that resulted in the Jesus Movement of the late '60s and early '70s. I was not interested in becoming a part of a new movement, but I did have a growing hunger to know God, to know Jesus, to know the Holy Spirit. I knew the Book rather well, but I did not know the Author intimately.

Almost two decades after receiving Helmut's card, while teaching in that college in Nashville, Tennessee, I was also preaching for one of the local congregations where a retired dentist often attended. Dr. Hall was a student of prophecy. He delved into the biblical prophets, Isaiah to Malachi, as well as the prophecy of the New Covenant Scriptures. One day after the service, he asked me if I had ever let the Old Testament prophets speak for themselves or had I just presumed that everything they had written had already been fulfilled at the first coming of the Messiah.

Flashes of Helmut's card! I had read the Bible for years, but I had read the Hebrew Scriptures only as history. In my annual reading through the Bible, I was always relieved to get to the New Testament. The ancient prophets spoke so often of Moab and Babylon, of Ephraim and Edom and I, not being an astute student of history, understood very little of it. Except for those occasional clear words that foretold Jesus' coming, I would almost speed-read the Prophets in order to get through them.

If I did run across something about Israel's return to the Land, I assumed that this was speaking of her return from Babylon. (Somehow I overlooked the fact that these passages mentioned returning not only from the East [Babylon] but also from the West and from the North and South—from the nations.) In those verses that told of the Messiah reigning over all the earth, I assumed the prophets were speaking symbolically and meant the advance of the gospel. If I did not understand a passage, I either ignored it or spiritualized it. "Israel" was the Church. "Israel's sins" were the sins of the Church. "Jerusalem" was a figure of heaven. "Zion" was another name for the people of God.

Stirred by Dr. Hall's challenge, I began to reread the Prophets. This resulted in more questions than answers. There was no place in my theology for a regathering of Israel. I had never even considered that there might be a time when most or all of the Jewish people would recognize their Messiah. I had been taught that Jesus would never again return to the earth. It never occurred to me that some of the prophecies might literally be fulfilled—that the Lord would again stand on the Mount of Olives and that the mountain would split in two, exactly as Zechariah saw it (see Zech. 14:4).

THE GREAT DEBATE

I was faced with a dilemma. What is to be taken literally in the Scriptures and what is mere symbolism?

I decided that I would rather assume that the Bible is literally true and then be proven wrong in that assumption than to assume it is symbolism and be wrong. I prefer to meet the Lord one day and say, "I took You at Your Word" than to meet Him and have to admit that I didn't think He meant what He said.

It seemed best to take the Scriptures literally unless the Scriptures themselves suggested otherwise. There were times when Jesus would expressly say, "The kingdom of heaven is *like*..." That's figurative language. Even in the book of Revelation, John often speaks of a "sign" appearing in the heavens (12:1), while at other times he speaks of seeing an actual new heaven and a new earth or a Holy City coming down from God out of heaven (see 21:1,2).

This literal approach to the reading of prophecy began to change my understanding of the Jewish situation. Passages that I had long allegorized now had to be more carefully discerned. For example, Ezekiel's "valley of dry bones" (Ezek. 37) is not just a good sermon to preach to a dead church, but it is exactly what the prophet said it was—a picture of Israel coming back to life (vv. 12,13). To accept the Scripture allegorically without accepting the actual prophecy is to thwart the full purpose of God's Word, to twist it to suit one's own agenda.

Once we have accepted the prophet Ezekiel's literal meaning—that Israel will live again—then we can apply that passage to other situations. This kind of openness to the Word of God keeps the Scriptures alive. The Lord, through His Spirit, continually brings fresh revelation, both the literal meaning and the spiritual applications.

We do not have the right to take words spoken to Israel and appropriate them to the Church until we have recognized their intended meaning to the people originally addressed. Even then, these promises belong to us, the Gentile Church, only because we are grafted in to Israel's roots and, along with her, inherit the promises made to her. Paul says that we have become a part of Israel's olive tree "among the others" and "share in the nourishing sap from the olive root" (Rom. 11:17). We do not replace the originally intended recipients. The promise of salvation is extended "to all Abraham's offspring—not only to those who are of the law but also to those who are of the faith of Abraham" (Rom. 4:16). Not only, but also! We join the family of Abraham and are "fellow citizens with God's people" (Eph. 2:19). The Jewish Messiah has become our Messiah. His blood has also redeemed us. We come alongside Israel in receiving the promises, but we do not *replace* her!

I was having difficulty in discerning the meaning of prophecy, not unlike most of the people in Jesus' day. The keepers of the scrolls did not understand their meaning. Those who were looking for the Messiah did not recognize Him. They were too preoccupied with preconceived perceptions of what the Messiah would do, of what He would be like. He stood before them in the flesh, but their eyes were closed. I was, in truth, no different.

The Scriptures were clear enough. Micah called Bethlehem the place of His origin (see Mic. 5:2). Zebulun and Naphtali in Galilee were singled out by Isaiah as a place that would see "a great light" (Isa. 9:1,2). Zechariah knew the price for which Jesus would be betrayed (see Zech. 11:12,13). Isaiah foretold that Jesus would be a suffering servant (see Isa. 53). Zechariah even wrote of a donkey that would be involved in His arrival (see Zech. 9:9). These predictions are crystal clear to us today, but the religious community of that day missed them completely.

"You diligently study the Scriptures because you think that by them you possess eternal life," Jesus told the religious leaders of His day. "These are the Scriptures that testify about me" (John 5:39). His implication is that they would have recognized Him if they had believed their own Scriptures. These were Bible teachers who were obviously reading not to learn but to prove!

THE REVELATION THAT COMES FROM THE SPIRIT

Intellectual honesty alone is not sufficient when we are seeking to know God. We must pray that our eyes will be open, that our hearts will be perceptive. We must yearn for insight and revelation. He not only speaks to the mind, but He also reveals Himself to the spirit. That revelation comes in His timing. We must be willing, but He is the One who reveals. We may read through Scripture again and again and miss the truth if our hearts and our spiritual eyes have not been opened.

Cleopas and his friend had a problem on the Emmaus road on Resurrection morning. They were looking into the face of Jesus but they did not recognize Him (see Luke 24:16). Not until the veil was removed from their eyes did they know with whom they were speaking. We need our veils removed!

Lydia had a similar experience at the riverbank prayer meeting just outside Philippi. As Paul began to speak, "the Lord opened her heart to respond to Paul's message" (Acts 16:14). Lydia had to be willing, but without that opening of her heart, she would not have been able to receive.

Do you see why Paul cried out to the Ephesians that "the eyes of your hearts may be enlightened" (Eph. 1:18) and that God "may give you the Spirit of wisdom and revelation, so that you may know him better" (v. 17)?

God does not speak a particular language. He speaks to us in our spirits through His Spirit. Revelation goes deeper than the mind. It impacts the entire being—mind, heart, intention, passions. This is why Paul told the Romans that their salvation had come by believing "in your heart" that God had raised Jesus from the dead (Rom. 10:9), that "it is with your heart that you believe and are justified" (v. 10).

LUKE 21 AND THE PRESENT-DAY MOVE OF GOD

It was this kind of searching that caused me to hear God's heart for Israel. The beginning of the revelation happened in the early '70s, when I was studying the gospel of Luke with a group of young people. Students were packed into a storefront classroom. They were sitting on the floor, Bibles open on their laps, hungry to know more of this Jesus whom they had so recently met. They had few preconceived ideas. They were reading the Bible afresh and asking the Lord for revelation.

For weeks we had been reading together through Luke's account of the life of Jesus, wanting to know more of Him so that we could become more like Him. The Lord was revealing Himself to us—both to me, the teacher, and to these radical young believers.

Everything was going along well until the week we came to Luke 21. I began to dread this particular class session because I did not know how to understand this chapter, much less interpret it to others. In this passage, the Lord had been talking to the disciples about the future—His future and the future of Israel. He spoke of the destruction of the Temple and the events that would surround it. But He also spoke of His own return. I was not always sure when He was referring to what.

I had read this chapter and the corresponding chapters in Matthew 24 and Mark 13 many times, asking the Lord for more revelation. I still grasped very little and yet I knew these verses were important for comprehending the times in which we were living.

JESUS SPOKE OF MANY SIGNS THAT WOULD OCCUR BEFORE THE END TIME. ONE SIGN IS UNIQUE TO OUR DAY—ISRAEL IS BACK IN THE LAND AND JERUSALEM IS ONCE AGAIN UNDER THE RULE OF THE NATION OF ISRAEL.

I was rereading the chapter one last time in front of my eager students when I began to see—on the spot—something pertinent to our day. The Lord was giving me revelation that has been foundational to my understanding of the times ever since.

Suddenly four verses seemed strikingly clear. Luke 21:20 surely speaks of the armies of Titus: "When you see Jerusalem being surrounded by armies, you will know that its desolation is near." The Roman armies began their assault of Jersualem in A.D. 68 and continued until its fall and the destruction of the Temple in A.D. 70. Jesus had wept over the city and the leaders' lack of receptivity.

Verse 24 speaks of the dispersion of the Jews. "They [the Jewish people] will fall by the sword and will be taken as prison-

ers *to all the nations* (italics added)." This happened just as Jesus
said it would. Many thousands died in the siege. Others fled the
city, never to return. They would soon be found in every nation
of the world. Some returned to Jerusalem a few years later but
were driven out again during the Bar Kokhba revolt of the 130s.[1]

After the Romans successfully crushed the Bar Kokhba campaign, Jewish people were banned from Jerusalem and from
Judea. Although there were times in the ensuing years when Jews
were allowed to live in the city and in the Land, there was no further serious Jewish occupation until the beginning of immigra-
tion in the nineteenth century. There was no Jewish state until
the United Nations' vote of November 1947 led to the establishment of the modern State of Israel in May 1948![2]

"Jerusalem will be trampled on by the Gentiles . . ." Jesus went
on to say in verse 24. And what trampling! Romans, Byzantines,
Muslims, Crusaders, Turks, the British—all have claimed time and
territory in the City of David, in this Land promised to Abraham
and his descendants.

"Until the times of the Gentiles are fulfilled!" I paused in the
reading, deep in thought. What a strange thing for the Jewish
Messiah to say. What could this possibly have meant to Jesus'
hearers that day? The Land had been in Israel's possession, more
or less, since the days of Joshua. Yes, some had been taken to
Assyria in 721 B.C. and had never returned. Others were held captive in Babylon for 70 years in the sixth century B.C. But even in
those times, Jews still lived in the Land.

Whatever Jesus meant by "times of the Gentiles," one thing was
clear: Israel's reentry into Jerusalem was strangely connected to
these words in Luke 21. As I read, the modern history of Israel was
merging with Scripture. The people now returning to the Land were
descendants of those who had heard the words I was now reading!

Jesus had said "until." I was suddenly confident that the "until" referred to the recent past when, in June 1967, the State of Israel held off six invading Arab nations and recaptured the city of Jerusalem. This was the first sovereign possession of the city of Jerusalem since 586 B.C., when the last Jewish king in David's lineage was driven from the city.[3]

In the margin of my Bible, I wrote "1967." If this Scripture had found its fulfillment in Israel's retaking of Jerusalem, then "the times of the Gentiles" also had meaning for our generation.

Sitting on the floor in front of me that day were not only Gentile believers in Jesus but also young Jewish believers who had accepted Yeshua (Jesus), the One whom Moses, Isaiah, Jeremiah, Micah, Jeremiah and the other prophets had promised. I had been hearing of an influx of Jewish believers like no other since the first century. Somehow I knew this was significant for our day.

I read on. In verse 28, Jesus said to His listeners, "When these things begin to take place, stand up and lift up your heads, because your redemption is drawing near."

I was having a "this is that!" experience—the kind of surreal moment that occurred when Jesus read from the Isaiah text in the synagogue at Nazareth. "Today this scripture is fulfilled in your hearing," He had said (Luke 4:21). I wanted to tell my young floor-sitting friends and all others who would listen to me since that time: "This Scripture is being fulfilled in our day!" I wanted to shout like Peter did on Pentecost morning, "This is that which was spoken by the prophet Joel!" (see Acts 2:16, *KJV*). I was experiencing what Jesus had declared!

The fulfillment of Luke 21 had begun. I was seeing the beginning of the end. I was to stand up and lift up my head, our redemption was near.

But what is "near"? I don't know. The Lord does not reckon time as we do. "Near" may be many years, or it may be tomorrow.

The last verse to catch my attention was verse 32. "This generation will certainly not pass away until all these things have happened." What generation? The generation at the time of Jesus? No, that cannot be, since that generation has long since gone. The generation that begins to see these things being fulfilled? I think so.

But how long is a generation? I don't have a definitive answer to that question, either. The Lord led Israel through the wilderness for 40 years and called it a generation. Yet He told Moses that the Israelites would come back to the Promised Land "in the fourth generation" (Gen. 15:16). That return took 400 years. So a generation could be 100 years. All I can say for certain is that He promised that all these things would occur, and I believe Him.

SIGNS OF HIS COMING

But wait, you may be saying. We are not supposed to be involved in date setting for the Second Coming, are we? Didn't Jesus Himself say, "No one knows about that day or hour, not even the angels in heaven, nor the Son, but only the Father" (Matt. 24:36)? Have there not been hundreds of prognosticators, all of whom have been proven wrong? Didn't Jesus say that His coming would be like a thief in the night? Are we not to live in a constant state of readiness?

Yes and no.

No, we are not to be ignorant of the "season." Jesus chided the leaders of His day for not discerning the times (see Matt. 16:3). "You . . . are not in darkness so that this day should surprise you like a thief," Paul told the Thessalonians (1 Thess. 5:4). "As it was in the days of Noah, so it will be at the coming of the Son of Man" (Matt. 24:37).

How was it in the days of Noah? Noah, warned of God, was not surprised when the rains came. He and his family knew that they were living in the season of the coming judgment. Though they had never experienced a flood, the ark was built and ready. The animals were coming. They knew the time was near.

According to Paul's admonition to the Thessalonians, it is the "people" who will be saying, "Peace and safety." Unbelievers have a false sense of security, but not believers. "Destruction will come . . . suddenly"—a point made graphic by Paul's vivid illustration—*"as labor pains on a pregnant woman"* (1 Thess. 5:3, italics added).

Labor pains come as no surprise to a pregnant woman. She has been expecting them for nine months. She still does not know the hour or the day of her child's arrival, not even when the pains will begin. But she knows that her time is near. This is how it will be at the coming of the Son of Man.

Jesus spoke of many signs that would occur through the centuries before the time of the end. Most of these have happened in every generation—floods, famines, plagues. They may be coming with greater frequency, but they are not new. They alone are insufficient clues regarding the season in which we are living.

Paul told Timothy that the end times would usher in a period of intense brutality, of civil and family unrest, of increased addictions (lack of self-control), a time when the whole world would be seeking after pleasure. Even the Body of Christ would have "a form of godliness but deny its power" (see 2 Tim. 3:1-5). These signs, too, have been present in former generations.

One sign is unique to our day. Israel is back in the Land, and Jerusalem is once again under the rule of the nation of Israel, just as the prophets and Jesus foretold.

When Jesus was predicting the fall of Jerusalem, He wept over the city:

> O Jerusalem, Jerusalem, you who kill the prophets and stone those sent to you, how often I have longed to gather your children together, as a hen gathers her chicks under her wings, but you were not willing. . . . I tell you, you will not see me again until you say, "Blessed is he who comes in the name of the Lord" (Matt. 23:37,39).

This word was not spoken to the Gentiles. It was spoken to Jesus' blood family, Israel. He would not return until the Jewish people were ready to receive Him. With the eyes of faith, we can see that time approaching.

Just this week I received a letter from one of my Jewish brothers in Jerusalem, who wrote, "More and more of us in Jerusalem and in Israel are crying out to the Lord, 'Blessed is He who comes in the name of the Lord!'"

Not long ago I personally stood on the Mount of Olives with a significant number of Jewish believers who gazed up into the sky and prayed, "Blessed are You, O Lord! You who have come, You who will come in the name of the Lord!"

No generation since the first century has seen such a rapidly increasing body of Jewish believers, both in the Land and in the nations. The "until" Jesus spoke when overlooking Jerusalem that day shortly before His death is drawing nearer. We are seeing Jews who are ready to embrace their Messiah—Jews who are ready to say "Blessed is he who comes in the name of the Lord."

Walk with me through some of the truths I have learned since that day with my hippie/Jesus Movement class of young Jewish and Gentile believers. Let me tell you about other prophecies that are unfolding before us—recorded words of the Prophets that looked forward to our day.

If you question what I am saying, take "my" Scriptures and test them for yourself. Open your Bible and read. Ask the Lord to open your heart and mind and spirit. Leave behind preconceptions of the biblical record. Let the Lord speak to you. Ask for revelation. Seek wisdom. Be willing to be changed!

My own focus is sharpening. God's heart for the Jewish people must be my heart for them. As our hearts turn with the longing He has for this specially called family, you and I will find ourselves under that age-old blessing spoken to Abraham, and our spirits will be quickened to read the global signs of the Messiah's imminent return to claim all of His children—Jew and Gentile alike.

Notes

1. A revolt against the Romans took place in A.D. 132, after the Roman Emperor Hadrian established a new city in Jerusalem and built in it a temple to Jupiter. The Bar Kokhba revolt is named after Simeon bar Koseva, later called Kokhba and thought by some to be the Messiah, who drove out the Romans. The designation *Kokhba* is thought to have been an allusion to the Numbers 24:17 reference to the "star" coming out of Judah, a messianic reference. The revolt was short-lived, ending in a Roman victory in A.D. 134. ("Bar Kokhba" and "The Bar Kokhba Revolt," *Encyclopaedia Judaica* [Jerusalem: Judaica Multimedia, 1997], CD-ROM.)

2. If the vote were taken today, it would be hard to find a single nation that would approve Israel's statehood. Even the United States is pressuring her to make concessions for peace with nations who have vowed to drive her into the sea.

3. There was one brief interval in 164 B.C. when Judas Maccabaeus and his forces controlled Jerusalem, but it was only a matter of time before the Romans returned.

CHAPTER 2

THE "GREATER RICHES" WORLD REVIVAL

If their transgression means riches for the world, and their loss means riches for the Gentiles, how much greater riches will their fullness bring!

ROMANS 11:12

I was never the same after my revelation from Luke 21. Although I continued to pastor a church, I remained alert to Jewish issues. I read every book, newspaper and magazine I could find pertaining to this subject. Israel was then, as it is now, almost daily on the evening news. My heart was irresistibly drawn to Jewish people. At times I was overcome with grief for this people who had endured the wrath of the nations for so many centuries. All my studies in many passages in the Scriptures, both Old Covenant and New, drove me to examine all data from this perspective.

We are told that over half of the people who have ever lived on the earth since the days of Adam and Eve are alive today. The latest figures indicate that one out of every five of these is a believer—more believers today than in all the years preceding us.[1] Millions of people on every continent are coming to faith—the greatest revival in the history of the world!

For example, 80 million Chinese are now Christians. Some believe that figure to be 150 million. According to YWAM's (Youth With A Mission's) latest figures, 1,200 people per hour are coming to faith.[2] That's over 10 million a year. Fifty years ago there were no more than 1 million believers in that vast country. Why? How can we explain such a dramatic increase in the harvest of souls?

In 1948, when the State of Israel was born, China, with its 1 million believers was about to come under Communist rule. Pastors and leaders were imprisoned or killed, and church buildings were destroyed. The Church was forced to go underground. But the Church did not die. By the time of Israel's Jubilee 50 years later, when Westerners were able to contact the underground Church, they found a thriving community of faith—80 million strong. That alone is an increase of 8,000 percent! What connection is there between this astounding statistic and the Jewish people?

Robert Leighton, a Puritan of the seventeenth century, came to understand that connection. He wrote,

> They forget a main point for the Church's glory who pray not daily for the conversion of the Jews. Undoubtedly, that people of the Jews shall once more be commanded

to arise and shine, and their return shall be the 'riches of the Gentiles,' and that shall be a more glorious time than ever the Church of God did yet behold![3]

These words, written over 350 years ago, posed a revolutionary concept in his day. For 17 centuries the Church had assumed that God was finished with Israel, that the Church had replaced her. The Christian Church was now to be the recipient of all the promises formerly made to Israel.

Leighton must have been reading the "Jewish section" of the book of Romans (chapters 9-11) when he came upon a series of searing questions written by Paul: "Did God reject his people?" (11:1). "Did they stumble so as to fall beyond recovery?" (v. 11). "If their transgression means riches for the world, and their loss means riches for the Gentiles, how much greater riches will their fullness bring?" (v. 12). "If their rejection is the reconciliation of the world, what will their acceptance be but life from the dead?" (v. 15).

Wait a minute! Robert Leighton must have thought. God is not through with the Jews! They are coming back. And according to Paul, when they do, it will mean the greatest harvest of souls the world has yet known! Greater riches! Life from the dead!

Leighton understood Paul to be saying that world revival among the nations would parallel Israel's return to the Land and to the Lord. Robert Leighton was seeing prophetically what our generation is now experiencing.

SEEING IN ADVANCE

Robert Leighton's voice was not the only prophetic voice of earlier centuries that foretold the physical and spiritual restoration of Israel. As early as 1560, among the great English and Scottish Protestant leaders who produced the Geneva Bible there was recognition of God's yet-to-be-fulfilled call on Israel. These men wrote in the marginal notes of Romans 11:15,25: "He sheweth that the time shall come that the whole nation of the Jews, though not every one particularly, shall be joined to the church of Christ."[4]

In 1649, John Owen preached before the House of Commons, foretelling a time when "this ancient people" will come to be "one fold with the fullness of the Gentiles . . . in answer to millions of prayers. . . . There is not any promise anywhere of raising up a kingdom unto the Lord Jesus Christ in this world but it is either expressed, or clearly intimated, that the beginning of it must be with the Jews."[5]

In 1839, Robert Murray M'Cheyne, a Scottish Presbyterian, traveled to "Palestine" and returned home to preach a sermon based on Romans 1:16: "I am not ashamed of the gospel, because it is the power of God for the salvation of everyone who believes: first for the Jew, then for the Gentile."

Charles Simeon, Cambridge preacher from 1782 to 1836, once became so carried away with the future of the Jews that when a friend wrote him the question, "Six millions of Jews and six hundred millions of Gentiles—which is the most important?" Simeon at once scribbled back: "If the conversion of the six is to be life from the dead to the six hundred, what then?"[6]

"The great event of Israel's return to God in Christ, and His to Israel," said Bishop Handley C. G. Moule, honorary chaplain to the Queen of England from 1898 to 1901, "will be the signal and the means of a vast rise of spiritual life in the universal church, and of an unexampled ingathering of regenerate souls from the world."[7]

Andrew Bonar (nineteenth century) believed Israel to be the "everlasting nation" who are to be life from the dead to all nations.[8] Count Zinzendorf, the spiritual leader of the Moravians in the eighteenth century, looked for wholesale conversion of many tribal peoples only after the Jewish people returned to the Lord.[9]

The great English expositor C. H. Spurgeon wrote: "I think we do not attach enough importance to the restoration of the Jews. . . . But certainly, if there is anything promised in the Bible, it is this. . . . The day shall yet come when the Jews, who were the first apostles to the Gentiles, the first missionaries to us who were afar off, shall be gathered in again. Until that shall be, the fullness of the church's glory can never come. Matchless benefits to the world are bound up with the restoration of Israel, their gathering shall be as life from the dead."[10]

These and other men and women of former generations understood Romans 11 to be pointing to a time when the nation of Israel would be reestablished and great numbers of Jewish people would begin to accept the Lord, while at the same time a vast revival would sweep across the whole world.

They were seeing in the Spirit what today is being manifested in the earth.

THE JEWISH HOMECOMING AND WORLD REVIVAL

Jewish people began returning to Israel in greater numbers in the nineteenth century and are still immigrating by the tens of thousands annually. The number of messianic Jewish believers and congregations is increasing rapidly. And the world is experiencing the greatest spiritual awakening in history. According to Paul (and those biblical students of former generations), these facts are inextricably bound to each other: Israel's homecoming—both physical and spiritual—and world revival. Watch how these events merge.

SEVENTY PERCENT OF JEWISH PEOPLE WHO HAVE COME TO FAITH SINCE THE BIRTH OF ZIONISM, OR OVER 50 PERCENT OF THOSE WHO HAVE EVER COME TO FAITH, HAVE COME SINCE THE FOUNDING OF THE STATE OF ISRAEL IN 1948.

Seventy percent of all those who have ever come to faith in Jesus have come since the first Zionist conference in Basel, Switzerland, in 1897. At the birth of Zionism—the movement that heralds the right of the Jewish people to the Land—the ratio of believers to unbelievers was 1 to 27; today that number is 1 to 5.

Seventy percent of those who have come to faith since the birth of Zionism, or over 50 percent of those who have ever come to faith, have come since the founding of the State of Israel in 1948. According to Ralph Winter and the Center for World Missions in Pasadena, California, the number of evangelical believers is growing 3.5 times faster than the population of the world.

While there were only 3 percent of Africans who called themselves Christian at the time of Zionism's inception, today over 50 percent identify with the Christian faith. South Korea was only

1 percent Christian in 1897, but it is now nearing 40 percent. The largest church in the world is the Full Gospel Church in Seoul, Korea, with over 700,000 members.

In India there are now 103 million believers, with a new church being birthed every seven minutes among the Hindus.

More Muslims have come to believe in Jesus since 1980 than in all the previous 1,000 years. Statistics from the Lausanne Taskforce on Evangelism state that while Islam continues to grow at a 3.2 percent annual rate, faith in Jesus is increasing worldwide at a rate of 6.9 percent annually.

In Indonesia an estimated 20 percent of the population is now Christian.

Consider also the birth of modern Pentecostalism (the rediscovery of the Spirit's work) and the birth of Zionism—the move to reestablish the State of Israel—both happening around the turn of the nineteenth century. The Latter Rain Revival, the great healing ministry that swept through the world 50 years ago, also occurred almost simultaneously with the birth of the State of Israel in 1948. The Six-Day War of 1967, in which Israel took possession of Jerusalem, is strangely the same year as the beginning of the Jesus Movement, through which so many Jewish young people began to believe that Jesus/Yeshua is the Messiah of Israel.

This great world movement is not sparked by one mission organization alone; it is the work of the united people of God. The psalmist spoke of blessing that would come when the Lord's family "live together in unity" (Ps. 133:1). Jesus Himself prayed for unity among believers so that the watching world might believe (see John 17:21-23). The promise of the psalmist and the prayer of Jesus is gradually coming to fruition. This awakening of the nations is happening through the united efforts of people from most of the major Christian groups.

The AD2000 movement to evangelize every nation and every unreached people group of the world now involves people of every denomination. It is accompanied by the greatest prayer effort ever launched in history. An estimated 30 million are involved in prayer movements, often united through the aid of the Internet and often by praying for the same people groups on the same day. There are prayer mountains in Korea and prayer centers around the world.

Bill Bright of Campus Crusade believes the Lord showed him that 2 million people would fast for 40 days to usher in the world harvest.[11] Stadiums are filling with worshipers. Cell groups and house churches are thriving. Global reconciliation movements are uniting believers. Denominational missions agencies and parachurch ministries are cooperating to see that the task is completed. In all of this and in spite of our continued weaknesses, within the Church today there is greater togetherness and greater passion for the lost than the world has ever seen.

This growth is unprecedented in the history of the faith and has come about parallel to Israel's physical restoration to the Land and a firstfruits harvest of Jewish believers in Jesus. It is truly life from the dead for millions and greater riches for the whole world—just as Leighton, Owen, M'Cheyne, Simeon, Moule, Bonar and others thought it would be. Just as the apostle Paul knew it would be!

SIGNS AND WONDERS

As in the first century, much of the harvest of the twentieth century has come as a result of the sovereign intervention of the Lord through signs, healings, angelic visitations and other miracles. Christian bookstores are filled with books and magazines verifying these phenomena.

A Baptist missionary in Yemen tells of tribal Muslims who had dreams about the Son of God and came to the capital city to find Christians who could explain more about this Man "who calls Himself Jesus Christ."[12]

In India, a blind woman named Madu had heard of the *Jesus* film. From her scant knowledge of the Scriptures, Madu remembered a blind man named Bartimaeus who had called out for mercy and was healed. *Does the God of Jesus truly work miracles?* she wondered. As she drifted off to sleep, she murmured, "I am a poor woman, and I need help, too."

Early the next morning her famly awakened to Madu's screams. Rushing to her bedside, they found her rejoicing. "I can see! I can see!" she cried. Word of this Jesus who could heal reached the surrounding villages and many responded in faith.[13]

In 1983, in a North African village located about 125 miles from Algiers, the Lord began to move from house to house, communicating through visions, dreams and angelic visitations. He did not rest until every member of this Muslim community had been introduced to Him. At daybreak the villagers began to tell their stories. In the days and weeks that followed, 400 to 450 of the villagers became believers in Jesus as the Messiah. As missionaries began to research the history of the village, they found that over 500 years earlier, a Spanish missionary from Majorca had been stoned to death on this very site. That missionary, Raymond Lull, had written that Islamic strongholds are best conquered "by love and prayers, and the pouring out of tears and blood."[14]

Missionaries arriving among the Fali in North Africa were greeted with the question, "Are you the messengers sent to tell us about the arrival of God's Son?"[15] For hundreds of years this people had believed that one day God would have a Son and would send messengers to tell them about the event. When they received the message, they would know that the end of the world was near.

In Mozambique, an old woman who was badly crippled, deformed and deaf gave her life to the Lord and was miraculously healed. She was the first known convert in the region. Over 50,000 people have come to the Lord as a result of the harvest that followed.[16]

Life from the dead! Greater riches! Jesus said, "This gospel of the kingdom will be preached in the whole world as a testimony to all nations" (Matt. 24:14).

If Robert Leighton, John Owen and the others were correct in their understanding of Romans 11:12 and 15—and according to the evidence of our time, they were—then the greatest world revival among both Jews and Gentiles is just ahead. This grand world awakening has only just begun. The people chosen to bring light to the whole world will fulfill its destiny. This nation of priests, who have blessed others, will yet enter into its greatest time of blessing.

Notes

1. This and all other statistics quoted in this chapter are taken from articles on world evangelism in the January 1993, January 1996, and January 1999 issues of *Charisma*; from Bill and Amy Stearns, *Catch the Vision 2000* (Minneapolis, MN: Bethany House Publishers, 1991); and from a teaching tape by Loren Cunningham (founder and for many years director of Youth With A Mission), speaking at MorningStar Conference, Charlotte, North Carolina, and released as MorningStar's tape of the month in June 1998. Loren Cunningham often cites the Lausanne Task Force statistics.

2. Floyd McClung, ed., *Light the Window: Praying Through the Nations of the 10/40 Window* (Seattle: WA: YWAM Publishing, 1999), p. 98.

3. Iain H. Murray, *The Puritan Hope: A Study in Revival and the Interpretation of Prophecy* (1971; reprint, Carlisle, PA: Banner of Truth, 1998), p. 75.

4. Ibid., p. 72.

5. Ibid., p. 100.

6. Ibid., p. 155.

7. Handley C. G. Moule, ed., "The Epistle of St. Paul to the Romans," *Expositor's Bible, A Complete Exposition of the Bible in Six Volumes with Index*, vol. 5 (Grand Rapids, MI: Wm. B. Eerdmans Publishing Co., 1956), p. 590, quoted in Michael Brown, *Our Hands Are Stained with Blood* (Shippensburg, PA: Destiny Image Publishers, 1992), p. 25.

8. Andrew Bonar, *Memoir and Remains of Robert Murray M'Cheyne* (1844; reprint, Carlisle, PA: The Banner of Truth Trust, 1995), p. 192.

9. John R. Weinlick, *Count Zinzendorf: The Story of His Life and Leadership in the Renewed Moravian Church* (Nashville: Abingdon Press, 1956; Bethlehem, PA: The Moravian Church in America, 1984), p. 100.

10. C. H. Spurgeon, quoted in Murray, *The Puritan Hope*, p. 256.

11. Bill Bright, *The Coming Revival: America's Call to Fast, Pray, and Seek God's Face* (Orlando, FL: Newlife Publications, 1995), n.p.

12. Howard Folz, "The Unfinished Task of World Evangelism," *Charisma* (January 1999), p. 50.

13. John Lindner, "India: Reaching Hidden People," *Charisma* (January 2000), p. 66.

14. George Otis, Jr., *The Last of the Giants* (Tarrytown, NY: Fleming H. Revell, 1991), pp. 157, 158.

15. Folz, "The Unfinished Task," p. 47.

16. Ibid., p. 49.

ISRAEL—A NATION OF PRIESTS

You will be for me a kingdom of priests and a holy nation.

EXODUS 19:6

Martha and I had heard of Corrie ten Boom and read of this Dutch woman's determination to give shelter to Jewish people during the Nazi reign of terror in Europe. When the movie of Corrie's life story, *The Hiding Place*, came to the theaters, we went to see it. When the film ended, we were so overwhelmed with emotion that we could scarcely leave our seats. We remained silent as we left the theater and drove home. Once there, we even went into separate rooms and wept until we could gain enough composure to process what had happened to us.

These were God's people, the closest blood relatives of our Lord. What a miracle that any of them were still alive! And to have maintained their national identity through 2,000 years without a homeland? Impossible! Except that God had miraculously kept them.

In a largely anti-Semitic world just 50 years ago, the United Nations had voted by a two-thirds majority to appropriate her ancient homeland for the reestablishment of the modern State of Israel. It could not have happened a year earlier or a year later. God chose a small window of time for the words of the prophets to find their fulfillment.

One thing distinguishes this people from all other families on Earth: God chose them as a nation of priests for the world. "Although the whole earth is mine, you will be for me a kingdom of priests and a holy nation," He told Moses as He led the Israelites through the desert out of Egyptian bondage (Exod. 19:5,6). Now Israel was to represent God to the nations until "all the ends of the earth will see the salvation of our God" (Isa. 52:10).

But it would not be easy to keep this fledgling people free from idolatry. Even while Moses was receiving God's instructions for them, they reverted to pagan practices when he stayed too long on the mountain. The people wanted gods like those they had known in Egypt—gods they could see and touch. Aaron tried a compromise. He took their gold, fashioned it into a golden calf and said, "Tomorrow there will be a festival to the LORD." In other words, "Let us worship God in the form of this golden calf!" It didn't work. The Lord would not accept the compromise. Three thousand Israelites died in one day (see Exod. 32:1-5,28).

When Moses finally came down the mountain with the commandments of God, the first three commandments had to do with Israel's faithfulness to the Lord. "You shall have no other gods before me. You shall not make for yourself an idol. . . . You shall not misuse the name of the LORD your God" (Exod. 20:3,4,7).

This essential faithfulness to the one true God became the cornerstone of Jewish faith and is still expressed twice daily by observant Jews, and weekly in every synagogue of the world in the words of the Shema: "Hear, O Israel: The LORD our God, the LORD is one" (Deut. 6:4).

THE NATIONS OF THE WORLD HAVE WORSHIPED THEIR MANY GODS, BUT ONLY ISRAEL AND RELIGIOUS FAITH BORN OUT OF JEWISH ROOTS HAVE MAINTAINED THAT "THE LORD OUR GOD, THE LORD IS ONE."

Israel was to remain a separated nation. For this reason, intermarriage was forbidden. Even Solomon, with all his wisdom, was ensnared by his foreign wives with their foreign gods. It was idolatry that brought about the ultimate demise of both the northern and southern kingdoms.

Speaking prophetically for YHWH, this God whose name is so sacred that most Jewish people would never attempt to speak it, Isaiah lamented, "I reared children and brought them up, but they have rebelled against me" (Isa. 1:2). This is God, mourning His lost and wayward children!

It was this uniqueness of the one true God—His insistence upon their faithfulness to Him alone—that was Israel's challenge. The Canaanites, the Egyptians, the Greeks and the Romans did not object to Israel's God as long as He was only one of many. But God had clearly stated, "No other gods." Israel was set apart to worship Him alone, to keep faith alive in Him.

The nations of the world have worshiped their many gods, but only Israel and religious faith born out of Jewish roots have maintained that "the LORD our God, the LORD is one."

A GOD WHO RESTS

The fourth commandment that Moses brought from his mountain encounter with the Lord set aside one specific day each week for worship:

> Remember the Sabbath day by keeping it holy. Six days
> you shall labor and do all your work, but the seventh day
> is a Sabbath to the LORD your God. . . . For in six days
> the LORD made the heavens and the earth . . . but he rest-
> ed on the seventh day (Exod. 20:8-11).

What a novel idea! A God who encouraged rest. A God who did not enslave His people. No nation had ever known such a God.

By observing the weekly Sabbath, the Jewish family would forever be declaring the virtues of a God who provides for His people. Economics were not to be the determining factor of their lives. If they would live in obedience to His commands, He would provide enough in six days so they could rest on the seventh.

Israel's God affirmed this commitment to His Word for 40 years in the desert. Each day the people were to gather manna for one day, but on the sixth day they were to collect enough for two days; there was to be no harvest on the Sabbath. Some tried hoarding manna; others paid no attention to the command of the Lord and did not gather any for the Sabbath. Both groups were forcefully shown that God would be faithful to His Word (see Exod. 16:4,14-20).

This Sabbath rest was not only for the Israelites but was also to extend even to servants and animals. And there was more. Every seventh year the *land* was to rest. The people were to trust in God's provision for that sabbatical year. "Whatever the land yields during the sabbath year will be food for you," the Lord had told Moses (Lev. 25:6). Israel was practicing what farmers were later to learn—that the nutrients of the soil can be replenished by allowing the land to lie fallow for a year.

A GOD WHO PROTECTS

No government of the world could compete with the government of Israel. Hers was a monarchy ruled by God Himself. When compared to the legal systems of the world at that time, this system was astonishingly superior in kindness and mercy.

The remainder of the Ten Commandments forms the bedrock for interpersonal relations in the family and in the community. "Honor your father and your mother. . . . You shall not murder. . . . You shall not commit adultery. . . . You shall not steal. . . . You shall not give false testimony. . . . You shall not covet" (Exod. 20:12-17).

These commandments, if obeyed, would revolutionize society. There would be no need for courts or prisons, no need for police or security systems. Parents would remain together and both children and the elderly would be cherished members of the family.

Additional laws upheld high standards of morality and personal righteousness. Provisions were made for orphans and widows, and there were guidelines to be followed when accidents occurred. No nation had ever been given such humane and compassionate laws. Yet knowing that the people would not follow these laws, God also allowed for their weaknesses and the age in which they lived, providing rules for indentured servants and slaves and rules for divorce and polygamy. In the times when Israel followed the laws most closely, national leaders came from great distances to observe (see 1 Kings 10:24).

In more modern times, Israel has had amazing health standards above those of her day. For example, in 1847, a Viennese physician, Dr. Ignaz Semmelweis, saw a dramatic reduction in the death rate of his patients when he began to wash his hands after examining diseased patients or after performing autopsies on those who had died. When he attempted to institute this practice among other doctors in his obstetrical ward, he was dismissed from the hospital. After several months, he was able to obtain a position in a hospital in Budapest. There, too, the mortality rate of pregnant women was remarkably reduced when Dr. Semmelweis made his unusual demands of his staff.[1] His secret? The good doctor was only applying the principles God had given Moses many centuries earlier (see Num. 19:11-14).

In the early 1900s, Dr. Hiram N. Wineberg observed that cervical cancer was nonexistent in his Jewish patients. Studies conducted in 1949, at New York's Bellevue Hospital, at Mayo Clinic, and in Boston in 1954 further substantiated the claim that wives of circumcised males had fewer cases of cancer than those whose mates were uncircumcised.[2] Almost four millennia earlier, God had given Israel a covenant sign that protected their women from disease.

God said to Abraham, "For the generations to come every male among you who is eight days old must be circumcised" (Gen. 17:12). Recent research has found that a newborn infant has a peculiar susceptibility to bleeding between the second and fifth days of life. Vitamin K, the substance that aids in clotting, is not adequately formed in the child's system until the seventh day.[3] What a remarkable "coincidence"!

GOD HAS SUPERNATURALLY PROTECTED HIS PEOPLE ISRAEL DURING THE PLOTS OF THE HAMANS AND THE HITLERS THROUGHOUT THE CENTURIES.

Leviticus 3:17 records the words, "You must not eat any fat." This dictate was issued to Israel long before the world knew anything about cholesterol. Fidelity in marriage was practiced without knowing anything about venereal disease. In short, the Lord told Moses, "If you listen carefully to the voice of the LORD your God and do what is right in his eyes, if you pay attention to his commands and keep all his decrees, I will not bring on you any of the diseases I brought on the Egyptians, for I am the LORD, who heals you" (Exod. 15:26). None of these diseases! What a promise!

Through the centuries, God has supernaturally protected His people Israel, not from disease alone, but from her enemies. As a priestly nation, she would perpetually live in a hostile environment. To assure Abraham of continued protection, the Lord spoke in a vision, saying, "Do not be afraid, Abram. I am your shield" (Gen. 15:1).

He shielded Israel from annihilation and assimilation during her 400 years in Egypt and brought her back to the Land. He kept her during the plots of the Hamans and the Hitlers throughout the centuries of persecution and reestablished her.

REMEMBRANCE AND PROCLAMATION IN THE FEASTS

To encourage His people and to proclaim to the world both His faithfulness and the coming righteous King, God ordered the observance of certain annual festivals. Israel, as priests for the world, was to instruct the nations through the story of redemption made clear in the enactment of their biblical feasts.

Pesach (Passover) recalled Israel's deliverance from tyranny and was an annual reminder of the horrors of oppression and the joys of freedom. The original Passover observed in Egypt—in which the blood of a lamb was sprinkled on the doorposts of Jewish homes so that death could "pass over" and spare the firstborn sons—pointed to the Deliverer whose blood would carry the sins of the people and through whom a whole nation of "firstborn" would be brought forth (see Heb. 12:23).

John the Baptist called Jesus "the Lamb of God, who takes away the sin of the world" (John 1:29). The celebration of Passover now becomes not only a remembrance of the exodus from Egypt but also a celebration of the Lamb who has come and foreshadows the ultimate Passover/exodus of worldwide proportions described in John's Revelation when only those who have appropriated the blood will be delivered (see Rev. 12:11).

The *Hag HaMatzah* (Feast of Unleavened Bread) begins at Passover and lasts for seven days. Jesus compared Himself to the manna that fell in the wilderness, calling Himself "the living bread that came down from heaven. If anyone eats of this bread, he will live forever" (John 6:50, see also vv. 41,50,58). Piercing, bruising, stripes—all descriptive of *Matzah* and of Jesus—are mentioned by both Isaiah (53:5,10, *NKJV*) and Peter (1 Peter 2:24). During the seven days of this feast, nothing with leaven is to be eaten. The leaven—the yeast that puffs up the bread—is a symbol of sin that must be eradicated and is a reminder of the haste with which the children of Israel had to leave Egypt. But the further lesson here is that we are all to remain in a state of preparedness as we anticipate our departure.

The Feast of *Bikkurim* (firstfruits) is, significantly, on the third day after Passover. One sheaf of grain was to be waved before the Lord in proclamation of other fruit to come. Paul tells the Corinthians that Jesus, raised from the dead, is "the first-fruits of those who have fallen asleep" (1 Cor. 15:20). Jesus' resurrection is the sheaf being waved before a watching world that speaks of resurrections to come.

Shavuot or Pentecost (Feast of Weeks, also known as the Feast of Harvest) rejoices in God's providential care. The first *Shavuot* occurred at the time of the giving of the Law on Mount Sinai. That Law was the precursor of another law and another harvest—the law written not on tablets of stone but on the tablets of the human heart (see Jer. 31:33). It was Pentecost morning, 50 days after Jesus' crucifixion, when the breath of the

Spirit blew through Jerusalem, inscribing this new law of love—law of life—on the hearts of the waiting disciples (see Acts 2:1-4; Rom. 8:1,2).

The fall feasts begin with *Rosh Hashanah* (Feast of Trumpets, literally meaning "head of the year"). The *shofar* (trumpet) is blown to usher in the beginning of the civil year and to begin the Ten Days of Awe from *Rosh Hashanah* to *Yom Kippur* (Day of Atonement). This is a time of introspection and self-examination as we anticipate the trumpet sounds that will announce the Lord's arrival (see 1 Cor. 15:52; 1 Thess. 4:16,17; Rev. 10:7; 11:15).

Yom Kippur illustrates, like no other singular day in Israel's calendar, man's sinfulness and the need for pardon. Early on this "atonement day," Israel would come to the priests, confessing their sins; the priests would confess to the high priest. Through the confession of the people and the priests, the animal symbolically bore the sins of the nations and was killed in place of the people. The high priest then slaughtered the goat for the sin offering (see Lev. 16:15) and entered the holy of holies, "never without blood, which he offered for himself and for the sins the people had committed" (Heb. 9:7).

This whole process of confessing sins was repeated with a second goat. The high priest was to "lay both hands on the head of the live goat and confess over it all the wickedness and rebellion of the Israelites—all their sins—and put them on the goat's head" (Lev. 16:21), at which point the goat was released into the desert.

Interesting! An animal had just been sacrificed for the sins of the people, and yet now the one bearing the "sins" was sent into the wilderness. How could this be? The writer of Hebrews knew the truth behind the symbolism. He called these offerings "an annual reminder of sins" and assures us that "it is impossible for the blood of bulls and goats to take away sins" (10:3,4).

Thousands of animals were slaughtered each year, each one a prophecy of the Lamb that was to come. Only He—this one Man, this sinless Man—could carry the human burden and take upon Himself the sins of all of Adam's family, freeing all who would accept His payment (see Isa. 53:5,10). This man was Yeshua, Jesus the Christ, the Messiah.

In His last supper with His disciples at Passover, Jesus, our Passover "Lamb"—(our "Atonement Goat," though this is a shocking thought!)—referred to the bread and wine as His own body and blood. "This is my body given for you. . . . This cup is the new covenant in my blood, which is poured out for you" (Luke 22:19,20).

For centuries now, when believers observe the Supper of the Lord, holding in their hands the elements—simple bread and wine—scenes of that last supper with Jesus flash before their eyes. For the discerning heart, every loaf of bread, every bottle of wine becomes a visible reminder of the body of Yeshua, of His blood that has saved us.

Five days after Yom Kippur is *Sukkoth,* the Feast of Tabernacles (or Booths), the last of Israel's major feasts (the other two are Passover and Pentecost), which every Jewish male was required to attend. This was the time of the final ingathering of the harvest, anticipating the immense harvest of souls prior to Yeshua's return. Through this annual feast, the people of God were made aware of their years of wandering and of the temporary nature of their earthly housing as, for eight days each year, the faithful dwell in a *sukkah* (booth). The apostle tells us that Jesus "tabernacled among us" (John 1:14, *KJV*). Our dwelling is also temporary. The greatest "housing"—many mansions—lies ahead!

Gentiles have never been required to observe these Jewish feasts. Yet, as we move toward the coming again of our Jewish Messiah, more and more of us are wanting to reclaim this part of our lost heritage.

BLESSING TO THE NATIONS

The Lord told Abraham that the nations of the earth would be blessed through his descendants. This has been fulfilled in amazing ways. The Jewish people have blessed the world in total disproportion to their number. The Jewish world population, though only one-fourth of 1 percent, has produced 15 percent of the Nobel Prize winners since the Prize's inception in 1899.[4] Even that number is astonishing in view of the millions of Jewish people who have been driven from their homes and often to their deaths.

Their contributions to the world have truly been a blessing to all the earth. In his book *What the Church Owes the Jew*, Leslie Flynn wrote,

> If an anti-Semite decided to boycott all the tests and cures discovered by the Jews, he would certainly open himself to a host of serious diseases. Besides refusing Jonas Salk's polio vaccine, he would also decline the polio pill by Dr. Albert Sabin; the test to fight diphtheria invented by Bela Schick; the diet regime of Joseph Goldberger which has fought pellagra to a standstill; blood transfusions made possible by the work of Dr. E. J. Cohen of Harvard . . . the Wasserman test for syphilis; the vaccine for hepatitis discovered by Baruch Blumberg;

streptomycin discovered by Dr. Selman Abraham Waxman as an antibiotic . . . ; chlorohydrate for convulsions discovered by Dr. J. Von Liebig; and vitamins discovered by Casimir Funk.

U.S. Jews are twice as likely to go to college as Gentiles, are five times more likely to be admitted to an Ivy League school, and are over-represented in the fields of medicine, science, law, and dentistry.[5]

The world of music, too, would be greatly diminished without its Jewish composers, conductors, pianists, violinists and opera singers. Eugene Ormandy, James Levine, Arthur Fiedler, Isaac Stern, Jascha Heifetz, Yehudi Menuhin, Jerome Kern, Irving Berlin, Oscar Hammerstein, George Gershwin, Artur Rubenstein, Paul Simon and Richard Rodgers are household names.

Similar lists can be compiled in the areas of philosophy, journalism, philanthropy, politics and sports.

John Adams wrote in a letter to F. A. Van der Kemp,

I will insist that the Hebrews have done more to civilize men than any other nation. . . . If I were an atheist . . . I should believe that chance had ordered the Jews to preserve and to propagate to all mankind the doctrine of a supreme, intelligent, wise, almighty sovereign of the universe, which I believe to be the great essential principle of all morality, and consequently, of all civilization.[6]

When Frederick the Great asked his chaplain for one reason to believe in God, the chaplain is supposed to have said, "The amazing Jew, your majesty."

Having so often been beaten down, driven from their homes, their wealth confiscated and their lives endangered, this Jacob family has consistently been elevated to positions of leadership in the nations where they have been dispersed. Threatened repeatedly with extermination, they have risen to bless the very people who have oppressed them. In all their suffering, their priestly role continues.

Notes

1. S. I. McMillen, *None of These Diseases* (1963; reprint, Old Tappan, NJ: Fleming H. Revell, 1979), pp. 12-16.
2. Ibid., pp. 17, 18.
3. Ibid., p. 20.
4. Leslie B. Flynn, *What the Church Owes the Jew* (Carlsbad, CA: Magnus Press, 1998), p. 1.
5. Ibid., p. 2
6. Rabbi Joseph Telushkin, *Jewish Wisdom* (New York: William Morrow & Company, 1994), p. 498.

CHAPTER 4

THE TARGETED ANNIHILATION

The dragon stood in front of the woman who was about to give birth, so that he might devour her child the moment it was born.

REVELATION 12:4

I will never forget the day I heard Marty Waldman tell what it was like to grow up as the son of Holocaust survivors. Marty's parents had escaped from a Polish labor camp just as World War II was ending. They went first to Germany, then to Austria, before securing passage to the United States, where Marty was born.

Marty was standing in front of me. Behind me sat Rudi Pinke, a German pastor to whom God has given a Jewish heart. Rudi carries the shame of a humbled nation and looks for every opportunity to love his Jewish brothers and sisters.

As Marty described the weight of the grief that still affects his family, he spoke in a voice choked with tears, "I know I need to go back to Poland someday . . . but I have not yet been able to do that."

After hearing those words, Rudi sprang from his seat, almost knocking people over in his eagerness to reach Marty. Taking the man in his arms, he said repeatedly, "I'll go with you, Marty! I'll go with you. We'll go together!" They stood there, locked in an embrace of love—the son of a Jew and the son of a German—a preview of greater days to come.[1]

I have had my own God encounters with Jewish people. One of them, Eitan Shishkoff, was a hippie farmer in the mountains of New Mexico when he met Yeshua. He explained to me what it was like growing up in an assimilated home in Southern California. He had become disillusioned with life and wanted reality. God was distant. He needed something tangible. So he gave himself to the soil and to the elements and found relative peace in his soul.

That all changed in one day. Eitan's peaceful community was shattered when a friend was murdered. There was no place to go with his grief. Soon after, two "Jesus people" showed up at Eitan's remote farm, describing the Messiah and His mission of redeeming humanity. While these young untrained witnesses were speaking, Eitan had a vision of the Jewish Messiah, Jesus, hanging from the cross, eyes blazing like laser beams which pierced Eitan's own heart. It was an experience from which he would never recover.

As Eitan shared his story, the words of the prophets were pounding in my chest—words spoken to Jews: "Then you will know that I am the LORD" (Ezek. 36:11). Again I was seeing prophecy fulfilled before my eyes.

Eitan and I became covenant friends that day—this West Texas farm boy and the California Jew, our hearts inextricably bound for eternity.[2]

THE PLOT TO DESTROY THE SEED

These examples of deep brotherhood between Jew and Gentile are the exception rather than the rule. Anti-Semitism is still the longest-held and deepest hatred in human history. This animosity had its beginning in the garden when God promised Eve that one of her descendants would crush the enemy's head (see Gen. 3:15). The weight of this man-hatred later centered in Abraham and his descendants.

God's call to Abraham has been a mixed blessing. Under God's supernatural protection, the Jewish people have survived, but they have had to endure the wrath of the nations. Since the time of Abraham's call, Satan has targeted this family for extinction. If he could destroy Abraham's descendants, he would thwart the purposes of God in bringing the world's Deliverer through Israel's promised Son.

After Jesus came, Satan continued his assault against the Jewish nation. He knew that the Jewish Messiah would return one day to a reestablished Jewish homeland and to both Jew and Gentile who are ready to receive Him.

In the meantime, the enemy continued to attempt to seduce Israel through idolatry so that she would no longer be able to serve the purposes of God. If that failed, he would assimilate her into the nations so that she would eventually accept their customs, and her witness to the world would be nullified. The evil one has lurked in every dark corner of history to stalk God's chosen people.

The barrenness of Abraham's wife, Sarah, was one of Satan's first attempts to abort the promise. Not believing that God could open Sarah's 90-year-old womb, Abraham and Sarah interfered with His plan by substituting her handmaiden, Hagar, to guarantee the promised heir. The results of this interference are seen in the ongoing hostility between the sons of Ishmael and the sons of Israel (between Muslims and Jews). But God did not need any help, and He later provided the child through Sarah, just as He said He would (see Gen. 18:14).

That son, Isaac, was 40 years old when he married his cousin Rebecca. For the next 20 years, she was barren. But Isaac prayed, the Lord heard and answered and Rebecca gave birth to twins, Esau and Jacob.

From the time God chose Jacob's family as the people of promise, the invisible enemy from the garden orchestrated many events and circumstances to try to eliminate them. If he could do away with this one family, all the people of the earth would not be blessed through Abraham and his descendants. God's Word would be proven wrong and Adam's children forever separated from Father God.

Already, within Jacob's immediate family, we see the battle lines drawn. Famine came to the land, a famine that could have wiped out the family. But God had sent Joseph to Egypt to prepare a place of refuge for them. The Lord used even the jealousy of Joseph's brothers to His own good purposes. "Do not be distressed and do not be angry with yourselves for selling me here,"

Joseph told them, "because it was to save lives that God sent me ahead of you . . . to preserve for you a remnant on earth and to save your lives by a great deliverance" (Gen. 45:5,7).

Things went well with this remnant of God's people as He poured out His blessings on them in the land of Goshen. Ultimately, however, there arose a pharaoh who realized that the Egyptians were becoming dangerously outnumbered. If he could kill all the sons of Israel, the race would soon be assimilated into Egyptian culture and forgotten. This decree appears to have come from the pharaoh, but a more sinister force was at work. Under the Egyptian tyrant's cruel regime, the children of Israel became captives.

In the ensuing years there were other miracles of deliverance—at the Red Sea, in the wilderness, at the crossing of the Jordan, at Jericho and other cities—all reminders of Israel's destiny.

Finally back in her own land, Israel underwent a 400-year cycle of idolatry and repentance before God chose her second king, David, as the bearer of "the seed." The Messiah was to be a "son of David." But from that day forward, not only the nation of Israel but now, specifically, David's house would become the focal point of Satan's schemes.

The nation soon divided into two kingdoms—the majority of the tribes breaking off to form a new nation in the north. Nine dynasties reigned over that nation in the next two centuries. But in the small southern kingdom of Judah, a descendant of David was on the throne. There were many wars and many attempts to destroy David's house, but none of the attempts succeeded. God was watching over His promise.

In one interesting six-year span, it appeared as if the enemy had won. Young King Ahaziah was killed in battle. His mother,

Athaliah, daughter of Ahab and Jezebel, known for their idolatry, set out to have all of the king's sons killed and to usurp the throne of Judah. She almost got away with it. Only one-year-old Joash was spared. An aunt hid him for six years. At the age of seven, he was brought out of hiding and declared king of Judah (see 2 Kings 11). Until Joash had sons, all of the promises of God—the promise given to Eve in the garden, the covenant made with Abraham and renewed with Isaac and Jacob, the vow to David—rested in his young body. If Joash had been killed, God would have been proven fallible. But God was not nervous. He is not only the maker but the keeper of promises.

Nation after nation attacked the Jewish people in the following centuries. Foreign powers ruled in Jerusalem—Babylonia, Persia, Greece and Rome all had their day. At times it appeared that the struggling nation would not survive.

Haman, the fifth-century B.C. "Hitler" of Persia, planned the strategy for Jewish annihilation in his day. It was a woman, Queen Esther, a young Jewess, who was the salvation of her people. Her story is recorded in the book of Esther and retold annually in the synagogues of the world at the Feast of Purim.

Two hundred years later, the Greek ruler Antiochus Epiphanes controlled Jerusalem. In his attempts to hellenize the Jews—to assimilate them into Greek culture—he actually offered swine in the temple, the epitome of desecration. Judas Maccabaeus led the charge against this pagan invasion and brought God worship back to Israel.[3] The event is commemorated in the annual Hanukkah celebration, known in the New Testament as the Feast of Dedication (see John 10:22).

All efforts to destroy this family of priests were ultimately exhausted, and God's timing was finally right for the Messiah to be brought forth.

IN THE FULLNESS OF TIME

Four thousand years after Eve heard in the garden God's promise of a Deliverer . . . 2,000 years after God's covenant with Abraham . . . 1,000 years after David's lineage had been selected, an angel appeared to a young Jewish girl in Nazareth and a child was conceived. Both Miriam (Mary's Hebrew name) and Joseph, her betrothed, were, as the prophets had foretold, descendants of Abraham, Isaac, Jacob and David. In due time a son was born.

During Jesus' lifetime, the battle raged on. Again and again, Satan tried to assassinate the King of kings—in the slaughter of the firstborn sons of Bethlehem, at the time of the Temptation (similar to the garden temptation—an attempt to bring this "second Adam" under Satan's dominion), and eventually, on the Cross.

Pilate, too, had issued empty threats. "Don't you realize I have power either to free you or to crucify you?" he taunted. To which Jesus replied, "You would have no power over me if it were not given to you from above" (John 19:10,11).

Days earlier, Jesus had assured His disciples: "I lay down my life for the sheep. No one takes it from me, but I lay it down of my own accord" (John 10:15,18).

The devil had used every weapon in his arsenal to prevent Jesus' birth, His fulfilled life and His resurrection—all to no avail. Not only had the Messiah been born, but He also completed the task for which He was destined. He had given His life for the sins of the world. Jesus' death was a voluntary act of submission to the Father's will, prophesied by the ancients: "He was crushed for our iniquities; the punishment that brought us peace was upon him. . . . The LORD has laid on him the iniquity of us all" (Isa. 53:5,6). Mission accomplished!

Now the strategy had to be changed. Word spread that Jesus' disciples had come and stolen His body from the tomb—that He had not risen from the dead as it was believed (see Matt. 28:12-15). And though He was seen by His friends, by the women at the tomb, by the men on the road to Emmaus and by over 500 witnesses at one time (see 1 Cor. 15:6), the attack on the bodily resurrection of Christ still runs hot to this day. Theologians through the centuries have circulated all kinds of theories about the Resurrection. The enemy of our souls knows what Paul also knew, that "if Christ has not been raised, your faith is futile; you are still in your sins" (see 1 Cor. 15:14). What a coup for the devil if that were true!

But Messiah has come. He died and is risen from the dead. He has ascended to heaven. His life has been authenticated through God's sovereign power.

THE CONTROVERSY CONTINUES

Why now the continuation of anti-Semitism on all fronts? Why would Satan still provoke hatred for the Jews? Why would he now need to annihilate them as a race of people? Why have they been a target for persecution throughout the world in every century?

Because our invisible but powerful opponent knows something that many Christians have not discovered—that the promises of God will not be realized if Satan is successful in destroying Israel. The prophets had spoken of her return to the Land. Isaiah was assured that her eyes would not forever remain closed (see Isa. 6). Paul was confident that a day would come when "all Israel will be saved" (Rom. 11:26). Jesus looked forward to the time when Jews would welcome Him to Jerusalem (see Matt.

23:39). Zechariah saw a period when the Lord would pour out upon Israel a Spirit of grace and supplication, a time when He would reveal Himself to her (see Zech. 12:10). None of this can come about if Jews cease to exist or even if they lose their identity. No, it is essential to the plans of God that this people and their national identity be protected. As the time for fulfillment approaches, Satan's fury will intensify (see Rev. 12:12).

WHY WOULD SATAN STILL PROVOKE HATRED FOR THE JEWS? BECAUSE HE KNOWS SOMETHING THAT MANY CHRISTIANS HAVE NOT DISCOVERED—THAT THE PROMISES OF GOD WILL NOT BE REALIZED IF SATAN IS SUCCESSFUL IN DESTROYING ISRAEL.

Remember, Paul assured his Gentile converts that God was not finished with Israel. He warned the Gentiles against arrogance. He reminded them that they were grafted in to Israel's olive tree. He spoke of the spiritual sap that comes from Jewish roots. He indicated that the Gentile Church cannot be holy in a complete sense without her Jewish older brother whose birthright she has usurped. He told the Gentiles that they were to make the Jews jealous through their love and faith (see Rom. 11).

And yet the Gentile Church has not only failed to protect the Jews, but she has often participated in and even initiated persecution. Why? The enemy is a deceiver, and the Church has been deceived.

Early in Gentile Church history, its leading scholars began to turn against the Jews. John Chrysostom, late third and early fourth century, gave eight "Homilies Against the Jews." He assaulted their character as murderous, greedy, immoral, vicious criminals. "As for me I hate the synagogue . . . I hate the Jews."[4]

It was Spanish "Christian" rulers, Ferdinand and Isabella, who exiled, tortured and killed thousands of Jews during the fifteenth-century Spanish Inquisition.

The great Protestant theologian and reformer Martin Luther became a hater of Jews by the end of his life.

> Their synagogues should be set on fire. . . . Their homes should likewise be broken down and destroyed. . . . They should be deprived of their prayer-books and Talmuds. . . . Their rabbis must be forbidden under threat of death to teach anymore. . . . Passport and traveling privileges should be absolutely forbidden. . . . Let the young and strong Jews and Jewesses be given the flail, the ax, the hoe, the spade, the distaff, and spindle, and let them earn their bread by the sweat of their noses.[5]

Gerhard Kittel, eminent German New Testament scholar, published a book in 1933 on the "Jewish Question." His counsel? That they should accept discrimination and defamation as their due as second-class citizens whose lot is to wander "restless and homeless on the face of the earth."[6]

The pogroms had their origin in "Christian" lands such as Russia and Poland. The origins of the Holocaust? Christian Austria and Germany, countries whose church ledgers were filled with those who had been properly baptized and confirmed.

The Church has been deceived, serving as a pawn in the hands of her enemy. If only Satan could annihilate the Jews or keep them from the revelation about the Messiah who has already come. What more effective way than to use the very ones claiming to be His followers in achieving that annihilation! Or even assimilation. The plans of God will be delayed as long as the Jews do not "come home."

The prophet Jeremiah said, "I will raise up to David a righteous Branch, a King who will reign wisely and do what is just and right in the land. In his days Judah will be saved and Israel will live in safety" (23:5,6). This prophecy had its partial fulfillment in the first coming of the Messiah. Its final fulfillment is yet to come. Judah has not yet been saved and Israel does not yet live in safety.

Jesus told the Jewish leaders in Jerusalem that He would return only when they received Him (see Matt. 23:38,39). According to Jesus' words that day, a significant number of Jewish people will be back in the Land and will have accepted Him *before* He returns.

Ten days after Jesus' ascension to heaven, the Holy Spirit came upon the gathered disciples in fulfillment of Jesus' promise. Thousands began to believe that day. First, there were 3,000 (see Acts 2:41), then 5,000—counting only the men (see Acts 4:4)! Yet another time, Peter told a group of gathered believers, "Repent, then, and turn to God, so that your sins may be wiped out, that times of refreshing may come from the Lord, and that he may send the Christ, who has been appointed for you—even Jesus. He must remain in heaven until the time comes for God to restore everything, as he promised long ago through his holy prophets" (Acts 3:19-21).

The restoration of "everything" the prophets had predicted was still to come. This was a *future* date of which Peter was speaking.

What was promised through the prophets? That Israel would be regathered from all the nations (see Jer. 16:14-16); that her eyes would be opened (see Isa. 35:5; Acts 26:18); that she would come to know the Lord (see Ezek. 37:12,13); that she would still be a light to the nations (see Isa. 60:1-3); that the wealth of the nations would be brought to her (see Isa. 60: 5,11); that Jew and Gentile would dwell together in peace in the Messiah (see Isa. 66:19-21).

Marty and Rudi; Eitan and Don; Jew and Gentile. Together in Messiah. Gradually, perhaps, but it is happening!

Though targeted for annihilation, God's priestly people still live. Israel's blessing to the nations thrives. The natural descendants of Israel and the grafted implants are a proclamation of God's faithfulness, a strange and wonderful togetherness. Where—and how—did it all begin?

Notes

1. Marty Waldman is one of the leaders of today's messianic Jewish community. He has served as president of the Union of Messianic Jewish Synagogues in the United States and is the spiritual leader of the Baruch HaShem congregation of believers in Dallas, Texas.

2. Eitan Shishkoff presently serves as the spiritual leader of the *Ohalei Rachamim* (Tents of Mercy) synagogue in the Kryot, north of Haifa in Israel.

3. Judas Maccabaeus, whose name is immortalized in the intertestamental *Books of the Maccabees,* assumed the leadership of the great Jewish revolt against the Syrian leader, Antiochus Epiphanes. In 164 B.C., Judas took the city of Jerusalem, purified the defiled Temple and instituted a festival of eight days, which became the permanent festival of *Hanukkah.* For one brief interlude, Israel had overthrown the Syrian forces.

4. Michael Brown, *Our Hands Are Stained with Blood* (Shippensburg, PA: Destiny Image, 1992), p. 11, quoted in Malcolm Hay, *The Roots of Christian Anti-Semitism* (New York: Liberty Press, 1981), p. 27.

5. Ibid., pp. 14, 15, quoted in Frank Ephraim Talmage, ed., *Disputation and Dialogue: Readings in the Jewish-Christian Encounter* (New York: Ktav/Anti-Defamation League of B'nai B'rit, 1975), pp. 34-36.

6. Ibid., p. 15.

THE EARLY JEWISH "CHURCH"

Salvation is from the Jews.
JOHN 4:22

When Shmuel Suran, a New York Jew, opened to the first page of the *B'rit Hadashah,* the New Testament, he was not prepared for what he found.

"The book of the generations of Jesus Christ, son of David, son of Abraham."

"My God! He was a Jew!" That startling statement would launch Shmuel on a search for the proof that indeed this man, whose name had been used to malign Jews for centuries, was Himself an Israeli-born Jew from Bethlehem, the City of David. Just as the prophets had prophesied. That He was and is the Messiah of Israel!

For over 20 years now, Shmuel has led a band of Yeshua believers in Jerusalem, praying that the eyes of others will be opened to receive the same revelation.[1]

What a strange twist this faith in Yeshua has taken during the past 20 centuries. The promise was made to Abraham, Isaac and Jacob, founders of the Jewish family, a promise later renewed to King David, that one of their descendants would reign over the nations forever (see Gen. 28:14; 2 Sam. 7:16). Yeshua fit the prophet's description in every detail and was hailed by thousands of Jews as Messiah. Many of the national leaders rejected Him, of course, but significant numbers of priests and other leaders did receive Him (see John 19:38,39; Acts 6:7).

Every aspect of His life was Jewish to the core: His circumcision, His Torah studies—He baffled the Temple leaders with His knowledge of the Scriptures at age 12 (see Luke 2:47)—His annual pilgrimage to Jerusalem for the feasts, His faithful observance of the Sabbath. In teachings and conversations alike, He constantly cited Moses and the prophets. Even when dying on the cross, He gasped out words from one of David's psalms (compare Matt. 27:46 and Ps. 22:1).

His whole life was spent among the Jews. Only on rare occasions did Jesus have an interchange with those not under the covenant. One day when a non-Jewish woman approached Him, He explained, "I was sent only to the lost sheep of Israel" (Matt. 15:24).

His death was not without the involvement of Gentiles—the Roman soldiers, Pilate, Herod. But most of those surrounding the Cross were the Jewish people who had watched and followed for the three years of His public ministry.

Resurrection morning at the tomb? Jews, except for the Roman guards who "were so afraid" of the angel that "they shook and became like dead men" (Matt. 28:4). The resurrection appearances during the next 40 days? Jews. On the mountain of ascension? Jews again—only Jews. The 120 in the Upper Room waiting for "the gift" (Acts 1:4)? Every one of them a son or daughter of Abraham.

What about Pentecost morning? The recipients of the gift were Jews. And Peter called the prophet Joel and King David as witnesses that Jesus was the manifestation of what these men had seen (see Acts 2:16,25). This Jesus is "both Lord and [Messiah]" (Acts 2:36).

JUDAISM FULFILLED

The 3,000 newly baptized believers, who soon grew to 5,000 and more, were not founding a new religion. They were simply living out the fulfillment of a centuries-old faith in the one true God who had made a promise in the garden, then to their ancestors, that He would come to deliver them and ultimately the whole world through them.

These new believers were Sabbath-keeping, son-circumcising, Torah-observant, feast-celebrating Jews who now celebrated Jesus as the one who brought meaning to it all. None of these practices ceased when they believed in Yeshua. They still frequented the Temple (see Acts 2:46; 5:12). They were often present at the normal hours of prayer (see Acts 3:1). Even after having been called before the Sanhedrin to defend their faith, they continued daily in the Temple (see Acts 5:42). Ananias, the man who baptized Paul, was a "devout observer of the law" (Acts 22:12).

Salvation, however, is not obtained by observing the law. It is a free gift of God through the vicarious death of the Messiah. Now they could understand why Isaiah had spoken of a "suffering" servant (Isa. 53:3). Even the feasts and sacrifices took on more meaning. Passover and Pentecost, the Day of Atonement and the Feast of Trumpets were no longer a deliverance of long ago and a holy law written on stone tablets on Mount Sinai. Rather, they were a recognition of the Messiah who has come, our Passover Lamb, and a law written on our hearts. Just as Jeremiah had predicted—a "new covenant" (Jer. 31:31-33).

This was not a new religion, this was Judaism fulfilled—filled full! Nor would these believers have answered to the name Christian. Not until Antioch (see Acts 11:26) was a believer in Yeshua ever referred to in this hellenized fashion. (The term "Christian" comes from *christos*, the Greek word for Messiah.) No, they were called "Nazarenes"—they followed the man from Nazareth (see Acts 24:5). They were said to "belong to the Way" (Acts 9:2). Others saw them as only another sect of Judaism (see Acts 28:22). Tertullus called Paul a "ringleader of the Nazarene sect" when he was making his accusation before Governor Felix (Acts 24:5). But the term "Christian" was reserved for a future day.

Peter's housetop vision at the tanner's house in Joppa and Paul's Damascus Road encounter brought major changes. Gentiles began to be welcomed into the family, and they did not have to become Jews to be accepted.

This was very confusing to a people who had kept themselves scrupulously separate for all those years. A Jerusalem Council had to be called. Some were vehemently opposed to this revelation. "The Gentiles must be circumcised and required to obey the law of Moses," insisted some of the Pharisee believers (Acts 15:5).

There was much discussion and many testimonies before a decision was made. Circumcision and law keeping were not necessary for Gentiles. However, they must be very careful to give up pagan customs and unacceptable morals that opposed faith in the one true God (see Acts 15:19-21). The Gentiles were in.

The profile of the body of believers began a rapid transformation. Many Greek names were added to the roster of believers: Gaius, Aristarchus, Trophimus, Theophilos. Cities like Antioch, Ephesus and Rome soon became centers of influence in the ever-expanding family.

Some of Paul's traveling companions were Jewish, some Greek. Timothy, with a Jewish mother and Greek father, was circumcised before joining Paul's team. On the other hand, there was no such requirement made of Titus, who was fully Greek.

Jews and Gentiles were learning to live together. A first! But what about Jesus' Jewish followers? Were they now freed from their identity as Abraham's natural seed?

ALWAYS A JEW

Paul's special assignment was to Gentiles (see Acts 9:15), yet he never lost his passion for Jews and he remained an observant Jew for the rest of his life. "I could wish that I myself were cursed and cut off from Christ for the sake of my brothers, those of my own race, the people of Israel," he told the Romans. "My heart's desire and prayer to God . . . is that they may be saved" (Rom. 9:3,4; 10:1). He was careful to let Gentile churches know that the gospel was still "first for the Jew" (1:16). When he entered a new city, his first stop was always at the local synagogue—in Salamis, Pisidian Antioch, Iconium, Thessalonica, Berea, Athens, Corinth and Ephesus (see Acts 13:5,14; 14:1; 17:2,10,17; 18:4; 19:8).

Even while a prisoner in Rome, Paul "called together the leaders of the Jews" and "explained and declared to them the kingdom of God and tried to convince them about Jesus from the Law of Moses and from the Prophets" (Acts 28:17,23). Some were receptive. Some were not. Paul told his nonbelieving brothers that he would now turn to the Gentiles to whom he had been specially sent, and "they will listen" (v. 28).

ALTHOUGH THE APOSTLE PAUL METICULOUSLY DECLARES THAT SALVATION IS ALONE THROUGH THE FINISHED WORK OF MESSIAH YESHUA, HE WAS A LIFELONG OBSERVER OF THE NOW-FULFILLED LAW AND PROPHETS.

Jerusalem was always in his heart. Luke tells of a time when after one of his long journeys, Paul was "in a hurry to reach Jerusalem, if possible, by the day of [Shavuot]" (Acts 20:16).

Although Paul meticulously declares that salvation is alone through the finished work of Messiah Yeshua (see Rom. 3:21,22), he was a lifelong observer of the now-fulfilled Law and Prophets. "I am a Jew," he told the Roman commander in Jerusalem as he was nearing the end of his life (Acts 21:39). "I am a Pharisee," he reminded the Sanhedrin (Acts 23:6).

"I believe everything that agrees with the Law and that is writ-ten in the Prophets," he told Governor Felix at the Caesarea trial (Acts 24:14). "I have done nothing wrong against the law of the Jews or against the temple," he declared to King Festus (Acts 25:8). To his Jewish brothers in Rome, he said, "I have done nothing against our people or against the customs of our ances-tors" (Acts 28:17).

Yet his loyalty as a Jew was constantly in question. Once when returning to Jerusalem, Paul was confronted with the rumor that he had turned people away from Moses and was telling Jewish believers not to circumcise their children or to live according to their time-honored traditions. In order to prove that he was still Torah-observant, Paul took a vow. He even paid the expenses of some of the other brothers so that everybody would know that there was no truth in these reports and that he was indeed still living in obedience to the law (see Acts 21:21-24).

Some have wondered whether Paul did this merely to keep peace among the Jerusalem Jews. If that were the case, it would make Paul out to be a hypocrite, acting one way while in Jerusalem and another way in Ephesus. Clearly this is not the case, yet this man of deep convictions did not try to enforce one culture on another, not even Jewish Torah culture. He insisted to the Galatians that salvation was alone through the finished work of Messiah (see Gal. 2:16), though he himself was Torah-observant to the end.

The apostle James in Jerusalem, when urging Paul to take the vow, was quite positive that he [Paul] "stay[ed] in line and [kept] the Torah" (Acts 21:24).[2] "Paul took this vow, not out of compromise, but out of a genuine desire to honor God through keeping Torah,"[3] says Russ Resnik, one of today's resurrected remnant. "Paul still walked in obedience to Torah, but he was not under Torah."[4]

OUR JEWISH MESSIAH

Paul made quite a case for the law, even though he had said, "Christ is the end of the law" (Rom. 10:4). The end? How? "The law is holy," he said (v. 12). "Is the law sin? Certainly not! Indeed . . . I would not have known what coveting really was if the law had not said, 'Do not covet'" (7:7). "The law is holy, and the commandment is holy, righteous and good" (v. 12). "Do we, then, nullify the law by this faith? Not at all! Rather, we uphold the law" (3:31).

Jesus had made it clear that He did not come to abolish the Law and the Prophets but to fulfill them (see Matt. 5:17). But the law has never been able to make one righteous. It is only through the Holy Spirit that the "righteous requirements of the law" can be fulfilled (Rom. 8:4).

Then what does Paul mean when he says that "Christ is the end of the law"? Perhaps David Stern, a messianic Jewish scholar, makes it clearer in his translation of this verse. Stern points out that the Greek word *telos,* here translated "end" can equally well be translated "completion, aim, purpose, goal, outcome, or consummation." Writes Stern, "For the goal at which the Torah aims is the Messiah."[5] Christ is the completion, the goal, the purpose, the aim, the consummation of the law!

Was this Judaizing? Was Paul's observance of the law Judaizing? No. Paul was not asking Gentiles to act like Jews. The Judaizers were those who insisted that circumcision and law observance were the means to righteousness or those who insisted that Gentiles observe

Jewish law. The finished work of the Messiah is for both Jew and Gentile. Salvation comes by faith in what Messiah has already done—His atoning death on the cross for our sins. Nothing more is needed. Not our sacrifices, not our works. Paul was therefore constantly reminding both Jew and Greek that God "saved us, not because of righteous things we had done, *but because of his mercy*" (Titus 3:5, italics added). Although Jewish believers may still be observers of the law, it is not the source of their righteousness.

This Jew/Gentile experience seemed to be working. The Jews had known that the Gentiles would one day come to faith in the one true God. It was an essential ingredient in Messiah's mission. Isaiah had foretold it: "The LORD says . . . 'It is too small a thing for you. . . . I will also make you a light for the Gentiles, that you may bring my salvation to the ends of the earth'" (Isa. 49:5,6).

No, it was no surprise to the Jews. They were simply surprised at the timing. After all, the Jewish Messiah was not yet reigning visibly in Jerusalem. Rome was still in control.

Then something happened that precipitated cataclysmic changes. The tension between Rome and Jerusalem escalated. Roman armies surrounded the city. The ensuing seige lasted two years, but ultimately the city was destroyed and the Temple lay in ruins.

Jewish believers who remembered the Olivet discourse (see Matt. 24, Mark 13 and Luke 21) fled across the Jordan to Pella. Their flight accomplished two things: It further separated them from their Jewish brothers who now considered them traitors, perhaps even in league with the Romans, and it further eroded leadership among Jewish believers. Some of the Gentile believers began to interpret the destruction of Jerusalem as God's final judgment on Israel. No doubt, they surmised, He was finished with His "chosen" people, and their promises now belonged to the "Church."

Sixty years later another historic event sealed the doom of the Jerusalem Jewish Church. The Bar Kokhba revolt of the A.D. 130s was defeated and Jews were forbidden to enter the city. As if that were not enough, Emperor Hadrian rebuilt the city, named it Aelia Capitolina and dedicated it to three pagan gods. Any believers left in the city were now Gentiles. They took control of the holy places and entrenched themselves as leaders in the Jerusalem Church.

There were still scattered Jewish believers in the Diaspora—those outside Jerusalem and the Land—until as late as the fourth century, even believers in Messiah in Jewish synagogues, but there was little of Jewish influence left.[6] It is not surprising then that the Gentile Christians understood them less and less.

By the time Shmuel Suran picked up his copy of the Jewish *B'rit Hadashah* in New York City many centuries later, the Jewish connection to the Christian faith was almost forgotten. Few even consider the fact that it is still a Jewish Messiah who even now sits at the right hand of the Father, interceding for us (see Rom. 8:34).

The Church has become so Gentile in its practice of faith that those of us who would reclaim a biblical Jewish expression are often considered a little strange—a small price to pay for the rediscovery of our Jewish roots.

Notes

1. Shmuel Suran and his wife, Pamela, live in Jerusalem. He serves the *Chazon Yerushalaim* (Jerusalem Vision) ministry.
2. David H. Stern, *The Complete Jewish Bible: An English Version of the Tanakh (Old Testament) and B'rit Hadashah (New Testament)* (Clarksville, MD: Jewish New Testament Publications, 1998).

3. Russell L. Resnik, *The Root and the Branches: Jewish Identity in Messiah* (Albuquerque, NM: Adat Yeshua, 1997), pp. 72, 73.

4. Ibid., p. 80.

5. David H. Stern was born in Los Angeles in 1935, the great-grandson of two of the city's first 20 Jews. He earned a Ph.D. in economics at Princeton University and was a professor at UCLA. In 1972 he came to faith in Yeshua; he received a Master of Divinity degree from Fuller Theological Seminary and did graduate work at the University of Judaism. Dr. Stern taught Fuller Seminary's first course in Judaism and Christianity, organized messianic Jewish conferences and leaders' meetings, and served as an officer of the Messianic Jewish Alliance of America. In 1979, the Stern family—his wife, Martha Frankel, and their two children—made *aliyah* (immigrated to Israel) and now reside in Jerusalem. Dr. Stern is the author of several books and the translator of *The Complete Jewish Bible,* as described above.

6. Ray A. Pritz, *Nazarene Jewish Christianity: From the End of the New Testament Period Until Its Disappearance in the Fourth Century* (1988; reprint, Jerusalem: Magnus Press, The Hebrew University, 1992) gives a well-documented history of these early centuries.

THE "GENTILIZING" OF THE CHURCH

God has granted even the Gentiles repentance unto life.

ACTS 11:18

Recently, while in Spain with a friendship group of Jews and Gentiles, I visited historical sites of anti-Jewish legislation and persecution in former years. In Granada we stood in the Ambassador Room of the Alhambra Palace, where Ferdinand and Isabella had signed the 1492 decree to evict Jews and confiscate their property.[1] Here we were revisiting events, confessing sins and asking for forgiveness on behalf of ancestors long dead, whose decisions have continued to affect us to this day.

These were very emotional gatherings, but nothing had prepared us for what we would see when, in Toledo, we rounded the corner of an ancient street and came upon San Juan de los Reyes. Hanging from the walls of this old monastery were the chains with which Jewish people had been tortured and killed five centuries earlier—stark reminders of a dark past. This was not an abandoned building. Grains of rice were strewn on the cobblestones outside the cathedral, where a bridal party had been celebrating earlier that day.

Why were the chains still hanging there? Why had they not been removed? Our small band was struck dumb. Embarrassed, ashamed and stunned, we bowed our heads and backed away. And yet in the throes of grief and shame, I remember a kind of numbness in my heart as if there were no way to emote deeply enough to express what ought to be felt at such a time.

Around the corner was a small park. We shuffled toward the area and huddled together, still in speechless consternation. Then one of our Jewish mothers sat down on the ground and began to throw dust on her head, her way of expressing the inexpressible. I sat beside her, following her lead. Others, Jew and Gentile, held each other. After a long season of silence, someone began saying *Kaddish*—the Jewish prayer for the dead—honoring the Jewish men, women and children who had been tormented and murdered by past generations of "Christians."

Back in the first century, the Jews had graciously received us as equals in the family. But we had rejected them. How had it come to this?

Paul, the apostle to the Gentiles, had begun to see danger signs in the last days of his life. "Do not boast over those branches," he had warned the Romans. "If you do, consider this: You do not support the root, but the root supports you. Do not be arrogant" (Rom. 11:18,20).

But arrogant we have been! Paul's admonition has gone unheeded for almost 20 centuries.

WHO KILLED THE MESSIAH?

By the time of Origen, about the middle of the third century, it was an accepted belief among most Christians that the destruction of Jerusalem and the dispersion of the Jews were God's method of showing the world that He was finished with them. They "will never be restored to their former condition. For they have committed a crime of the most unhallowed kind, in conspiring against the Saviour of the human race," Origen wrote in *Against Celsus.*[2]

What had happened to Romans 11:1 and 11? "Did God reject his people? By no means! Did they stumble so as to fall beyond recovery? Not at all!" And what about Jeremiah? Had Origen and others overlooked his prophecy that Israel would be a nation as long as the sun is in the sky (see Jer. 31:35-37)?

Did Jews *alone* "conspire against the Savior"? Was it not Pilate, a Gentile, who had to give the last word? And what about the Roman soldiers? Following orders? Yes. But actively involved in His arrest, torture and crucifixion.

Nonetheless, the Church was not taking any chances. Emperor Constantine called the Nicene Council in A.D. 325 to solve some of the doctrinal problems, but he also wanted to make sure that the Church had once and for all separated herself from these "polluted wretches" who had stained their hands with "a nefarious crime."[3] They needed a resurrection celebration date other than Passover. Passover was too Jewish!

"It appeared an unworthy thing that in the celebration of this most holy feast, we should follow the practice of the Jews, who have impiously defiled their hands with an enormous sin, and are, therefore, deservedly afflicted with blindness of soul," wrote Constantine to the assembled bishops in Nicea.[4]

At the conclusion of the Council meeting, Constantine had his way and celebrated with a huge church banquet. The Roman calendar had conquered. The annual celebration of the Lord's resurrection would now have a new name—Easter—strangely similar to *Eostre*, the Teutonic goddess of spring, dissimilar to *Pesach* or Passover, the festival of its origin. God's calendar for the Passover was subjugated by the Western Church from that point forward.

The prophet Daniel had envisioned four great beasts and a king that would "change the set times and the laws" (Dan. 7:25). In his insistence that the Church change the calendar of God, Constantine became a foreshadowing of another world ruler who is to come. And the Church was further estranged from her roots and her spiritual "parents."

"It is into their place that ye have been set," John Chrysostom assured his flock a few years later.[5] Jewish people who had come to faith were now expected to renounce everything Jewish. If they refused, they were considered heretics and came under the ire of a confused Gentile Church.

Further generations of theologians accepted the "replacement theory" as doctrine.[6] Jeremiah and Paul were forgotten; their clear words reinterpreted.

By the time of the Second Nicene Council in A.D. 787, believing Jews had to prove they were "Christians." They were, for example, refused Communion by decree of the Church Council unless they forsook the observance of the Sabbath or any other Jewish custom. In some cases they had to prove their disdain for their roots by eating pork in front of witnesses.[7]

The Lateran councils of A.D. 1179 and A.D. 1215 ordered Jews to live in separate quarters and to wear distinctive dress. This paved the way for ghetto living and the yellow badge required prior to and during the time of the Nazi Holocaust.

Martin Luther brought hope to millions through the Reformation movement of the sixteenth century. Paul's letter to the Romans had brought him life. But Luther seems to have gleaned nothing from Romans 11:28,29: "As far as the gospel is concerned, they [the Jews] are enemies on your account; but as far as election is concerned, they are loved on account of the patriarchs, for God's gifts and his call are irrevocable." Luther's comments? "The word 'enemies' must here be taken in a passive sense, that is, they [the Jews] deserve to be hated. God hates them, and so they are hated by the Apostles and all who are of God."[8]

God hates them? Just the opposite. Rather, Paul says, "They are loved." Earlier in the same chapter, Paul says that they are not rejected. They have not fallen beyond recovery. They will rise again. It will be a time of great riches.

As much as Luther did to bring about a reformed Church, he helped advance further disdain for this chosen family of God. Years later, Hitler did not have to look far to find justification for his hatred of the Jews. Luther is quoted in the evil dictator's classic work *Mein Kampf!*

During these years there was no place of safety for a Jewish believer. Either he kept quiet about his faith and remained in his local synagogue—thus denying his Lord—or he acknowledged his faith and was forced out of the Jewish fellowship into the strange world of the Gentiles, losing all future identity as a Jew.

I wonder, too, about the people who once hung from those chains on the side of San Juan de los Reyes. Were they Jews who had been forced to pledge allegiance to an invisible king they did not even know? Or were they Jewish believers who had refused to give up being Jewish? I can close my eyes and still see them. Silent, gruesome witnesses of a fallen Church.

As for who killed the Messiah? The sins of Adam's entire family were on Messiah's shoulders that day on the cross. Our sins nailed Him there. He came to redeem both Jew and Gentile, and it was both Jew and Gentile who condemned Him to death.

THE ESTRANGEMENT CONTINUES

In our own century, the idea that the Church has replaced Israel has so permeated our thinking that even recently published Bibles often contain marginal notes and chapter headings that continue to support this ancient error that results in hatred of Jews.

One well-known Bible dictionary, in commenting on Paul and his relationship to his Jewishness, states:

Paul argued that the Jews had forfeited these promises, which had come to Abraham through faith, not the law (Rom. 4:13). Because "it is men of faith who are the [true] sons of Abraham" (Gal. 3:7), Christians, not Jews, could now claim to be descended from the Israelite patriarchs. The Church was, in fact "the twelve tribes in the Dispersion" (Jas. 1:1)."[9]

In this excellent dictionary the words of Paul have been used to declare what Paul had clearly denied—that the Gentiles have replaced Israel. Paul was indeed insisting that it is faith, not self-righteous adherence to the law, that saves. But in no place does he or James call Gentiles "the twelve tribes in the Dispersion."

THE IDEA THAT THE CHURCH HAS REPLACED ISRAEL HAS SO PERMEATED OUR THINKING THAT EVEN RECENTLY PUBLISHED BIBLES OFTEN SUPPORT THIS ANCIENT ERROR THAT RESULTS IN HATRED OF JEWS.

One study Bible,[10] in all other points a fine work, points out the widespread acceptance of the spiritual demise of Israel and the ascendancy of the Church. For example, the chapter headings for Isaiah read:

Isaiah 41—*God speaks of his merciful providence in regard to his church*
Isaiah 43—*The Lord comforts the church with his promises*
Isaiah 52—*The church roused with God's promise of free redemption*
Isaiah 60—*Glory of the church in the abundant access of the Gentiles*
Isaiah 65—*The Gentiles called. The Jews rejected. A remnant saved. Blessed state of the new Jerusalem.*

The headings at the top of pages make this emphasis even more obvious:

God's mercies to the church
God's promises to the church
The restoration of the church
The prophet's zeal for the church
Confession and complaint of the church

With these constant references to the Church, even though the Church is never mentioned in any of these chapters, the real subject of Israel is overlooked.

Listen to this statement from another of today's writers: "'The nation that will not serve us will perish' (Isa. 60:12); 'all the peoples of the earth will be subdued under our feet' (Ps. 47:1-3)— promises made originally to Israel, but now to be fulfilled in the New Israel, the Church."[11]

The promises made to Israel are indeed available to Gentiles, but only as they come into covenant with and partner with redeemed Israel. Paul makes it very plain that those who were Gentiles by birth and separated from Christ, "excluded from citizenship in Israel and foreigners to the covenants of the promise" had been *included* through the blood of Messiah. "Consequently, you are no longer foreigners and aliens, but fellow citizens with God's people and members of God's household" (Eph. 2:12,19).

We Gentiles have become citizens of Israel. That is our only access to Israel's promises. Once we were "foreigners to the covenants of the promise," but that day is past. Israel's Messiah is now our Messiah.[12]

We have made it difficult for the Jewish people to receive Him. We make demands that hold them back. The history of confusion is very long, the wounds very deep.

One group of modern theologians thinks we should no longer desire to tell the Jews about Jesus. These scholars have developed a whole new theology—a so-called "Dual Covenant"—the idea that the Jews do not need Jesus, that they are saved through their covenant with Abraham and that only the Gentiles are saved through Jesus.

What a travesty!

It is not enough that we have turned our backs on these closest of kin to Jesus. Now we have decided they do not need their own Messiah!

That is no answer. Jesus is Messiah of both Jew and Gentile or He is not Messiah at all.

Any true Christian deplores contrived conversions and manipulative witnessing techniques. We abhor intimidation. We grieve over our past. But yes, the Jewish people still need a Savior, as do we. We love the Jews. We bless them. We protect them in persecution. We make no demands of them. But He is their Messiah too. We dare not forget that fact.

"Jerusalem will be trampled on by the Gentiles until the times of the Gentiles are fulfilled" (Luke 21:24)! Prophetic words indeed. Yet none of Jesus' hearers could have imagined what would transpire over the next years: that the Gentiles would take control of the books of Moses and the Prophets—so much so that the Bible, God's inspired Word, would be appropriated by Gentiles for themselves to the extent that it is now known primarily as a Gentile book; that this Man in whom they now believed, this Messiah, this Christ, would become so "Gentilized" that even His own people would fail to recognize Him as one of their own; that millions of Jews in the twentieth century would be killed at the hands of those who gave lip service to their Messiah.

Yeshua, Son of David, Son of God, had now become Jesus Christ, Savior of the Gentiles. In earlier times, the Jews had received us into their family, but we now rejected them. In the heart of the Church, the Gentiles were in but the Jews were out.

The Church assumed that all was well, but the Lord was not pleased with the rejection. There was a price to be paid. The people who had rejected God's choice family would not even find unity among themselves.

Notes

1. "Isabella I," *Encarta Encyclopedia*, 1998, CD-ROM.
2. Origen, *Against Celsus*, quoted in Ray A. Pritz, *Nazarene Jewish Christianity, From the End of the New Testament Period Until Its Disappearance in the Fourth Century* (1988; reprint, Jerusalem: Magnus Press, The Hebrew University, 1992), p. 21.
3. Constantine, quoted in Dan Gruber, *The Church and the Jews* (Hanover, NH: Elijah Publishing, 1997), p. 35.
4. Ibid.
5. John Chrysostom, *Homilies on the Acts of the Apostles and the Epistle to the Romans*, from *A Select Library of the Nicene and Post-Nicene Fathers of the Christian Church*, vol. 11, ed. Philip Schaff (New York: The Christian Literature Company, 1889), p. 491.
6. Replacement Theology is the belief that God is finished with Israel and that the Gentile Church has now replaced her, that there is no future role for Israel and the Jewish people.
7. Canon VIII from the Second Nicene Council.
8. Martin Luther, *Commentary on the Epistle to the Romans*, trans. J. Theodore Mueller (Grand Rapids, MI: Zondervan Publishing House, 1954), n.p.
9. *Harper's Bible Dictionary*, 1985, s.v. "Israel."
10. *Thompson Chain Reference Bible*, 4th improved ed. (Indianapolis, IN: B. B. Kirkbride Company, 1964).
11. David Chilton, *The Days of Vengeance: An Exposition of the Book of Revelation* (Fort Worth, TX: Dominion Press, 1984), p. 117.
12. One of the passages of Scripture occasionally mentioned in support of "Replacement Theology"—the belief that the Church has now replaced Israel—is in the conclusion of Paul's letter to the Galatians (6:16). In Paul's benediction, he says, "Peace and mercy to all who follow this rule, even to the Israel of God." The argument is that Paul is here referring to the

Church as "the Israel of God." As a replacement for Israel? Who says? How does the "Israel of God" suddenly mean the Church when it has meant the "Israel of God" since the days of Abraham, Isaac and Jacob!

At the very most, Paul may be including believing Gentiles, since he has assured the Roman believers that Gentiles are grafted in to the Jewish olive root (see Rom. 11:17,18). In his letter to the Romans, he is adamant that they have not replaced but share in the Jewish root (see Rom. 11:11-24). Now in this Galatian letter, Paul is continually emphasizing that law never has and never will save, that salvation and sanctification come through the finished work of the Messiah through the Holy Spirit, and that the Gentiles have never been placed under the same Mosaic requirements as Israel. But never does he suggest that God is finished with Israel.

After writing an entire letter warning against those who would require Gentiles to be Torah-observant (see Gal. 2:13,14) or even make Torah-observance a saving factor for Jews (see vv. 15,16), he concludes by saying neither circumcision nor uncircumcision means anything; what counts is a new creation (see Gal. 6:15). In other words, it's not Jewishness and Gentileness that save; it is the blood of Messiah.

Listen carefully to his benediction once again: "Peace and mercy to all who follow this rule" (Gal. 6:16). Who are those who follow this rule? They are both the Gentile believers and Jewish believers—all who have come to faith through Messiah's finished work at the cross. But Paul's prayer for peace and mercy goes beyond only those who are already following this rule.

In true Jewish poetic style, he expands on his initial remarks. He is thinking of those who have yet to acknowledge their Messiah. He may be remembering the psalmist's admonition to "pray for the peace of Jerusalem" (Ps. 122:6) as he ponders the fate of his own countrymen. Isaiah's words—reminding all who call on the Lord to give themselves no rest and to give the Lord no rest until Jerusalem is established and made the praise of the earth—may be pulsating through his heart as he adds that final phrase "even to the Israel of God." As a called apostle to the Gentiles, he may also be thinking of the countless Gentiles who will be grafted in to the family by faith, sharing in the promises of Abraham through Israel's Promised Redeemer.

But in no way does Paul intimate that God is through with Israel and that the Church has taken her place. Nothing in Galatians or Romans or any of Paul's letters—or the letters of the other apostles, for that matter—can be so construed unless we have been culturally trained to think this way. May the Word speak for itself.

CHAPTER 7

DIVISION—THE DNA OF THE GENTILE CHURCH

A man reaps what he sows.

GALATIANS 6:7

The early believers "were together and had everything in common" (Acts 2:44). They were "one in heart and mind" (4:32). In the Garden of Gethsemane, Jesus prayed that all of us may be one so "that the world may believe that you have sent me" (John 17:21).

But we are *not* one. There are now over 160 different ecclesiastical traditions with 23,300 separate and distinct denominations within the larger Body of Christ![1]

BY BREAKING FROM THOSE WHO BIRTHED US, THE CHURCH HAS PRODUCED ONE DIVISION AFTER ANOTHER. EVERY NEW MOVEMENT HAS RESULTED IN A NEW CHURCH; EACH REFORMATION, A NEW DENOMINATION.

The natural law inherent in all of God's creation—the DNA, so to speak—has had its effect on the Church. We have reproduced "according to our kind" (see Gen. 1:11). By breaking from those who birthed us, the Church has produced one division after another. Every new movement has resulted in a new church; each reformation, a new denomination. Nineteen centuries later we have: Eastern Orthodox and Roman Catholic; Anglican and Protestant; Calvinism and Arminianism; Lutheran, Baptist, Methodist, Nazarene and Pentecostal; denominationalism and nondenominationalism.

There was still a family resemblance, but a mutation had entered our bloodstream. Mutations may produce only a slight change in the first generation but can ultimately bring about "great changes such as severe deformities or diseases."[2]

It all began with that first break when the Gentile Church assumed a superior position. According to Marty Waldman:

The gaping wound of the schism between Jews and Gentiles represents the "granddaddy" of all wounds in the Body of Messiah. All other wounds of division in the Church stem from this original wound. Because the Church had grown to believe that it superseded Israel and Messianic Judaism, the spirit of supersessionism has plagued Christianity through the ages. The Orthodox Church believes that the Roman Catholic Church is in rebellion. The Roman Catholic Church has always viewed the Protestants as religious rebels. The many denominations and divisions in the Protestant Church are primarily the result of one group of Christians superseding an existing group because they have found a "more pure way." Supersessionism essentially nullifies the promise of God to the previous group.[3]

It was Moses who first heard God say, "Israel is my firstborn son" (Exod. 4:22). A firstborn son has an irreplaceable position of honor in the family. Paul was specifically speaking of Israel when he said, "God's gifts and his call are irrevocable" (Rom. 11:29).

GENTILE CHRISTIANS—THE STAY-AT-HOME SON

In the Gospel of Luke, Jesus tells the story of the Prodigal Son, in which the younger son leaves home, goes into a foreign country and squanders his inheritance (see Luke 15:11-31). Much later he "came to his senses" and started home. "But while he was still a long way off, his father saw him and was filled with compassion for him; he ran to his son, threw his arms around him and kissed him" (v. 20). There was a royal celebration. "This son of mine was dead and is alive again," the father rejoiced (v. 24).

But the older son was irate. His brother had lost his inheritance and that should be the end of it. There was certainly no cause for feasting. This younger rebel brother had gotten what he deserved in the pigsty of the "far country." Now everything should belong to *him,* the faithful older son. *"I've* been the one who has slaved for you all these years and never disobeyed your orders," he reminded their father, "and you've never thrown a big party for *me!"* (v. 29, author's paraphrase).

The Gentile saga is this story in reverse. The firstborn son, Israel, left home. The older brother, the Gentiles, stayed with the Father. As far as they were concerned, the firstborn was disowned and now to be regarded as an enemy. The son who remained at home assumed he had supplanted the missing brother in all matters, including the place of intimate fellowship with the Father.

After centuries of wandering, Israel is finally on the way home, but the Church is not happy. "They had their chance," we seem to be saying. "They squandered their inheritance. Now it's our time. They no longer have any rights in Father's house."

On the other hand, Father is saying, "Quick! Bring the best robe and put it on him. Put a ring on his finger and sandals on his feet. Bring the fattened calf and kill it. Let's have a feast and celebrate" (vv. 22,23).

Eitan Shishkoff and I once shared an unforgettable moment that has further bonded us in our mutual covenant of faith. Having been asked to speak to a messianic Jewish conference, we were both seated on the platform.

Eitan rose, made his remarks and sat down. While I was addressing this predominantly Jewish crowd, encouraging both

Jewish believers to keep the vision and Gentiles to stand along-side their new brothers and sisters in Yeshua, the familiar para-ble of the Prodigal Son—with a surprising twist—surfaced in my consciousness. Suddenly I saw myself as the "stay-at-home" Gentile, the son of the Church, who has maligned, ridiculed, persecuted and rejected her brother Israel. With crushing inten-sity, I felt the massive burden of guilt for generations of my ancestors.

In this moment of awakening, I also saw Eitan as the son of the persecuted race. It was so clear to me that he must always be bearing the grief of millions of relatives annihilated through the centuries. Reaching back, I drew him forward, then fell on my knees at his feet, shaking and sobbing. "Forgive us! Forgive us!" I cried, the sins of those centuries on my shoulders.

We Gentiles are the spiritual descendants of the Jewish peo-ple. "Salvation is from the Jews," Jesus told the Samaritan woman at the well (John 4:22). He—the Jew—is our "parent" in the faith. Without Jewish faith, there would be no Christianity.

It occurred to me one day as I was rereading the Ten Commandments in light of this issue that there may be more than meets the eye in the fifth commandment (Deut. 5:16): "Honor your father and your mother," the Lord commanded— "which is the first commandment with a promise," Paul adds in his letter to the Ephesians (6:2). Why? "That it may go well with you and that you may enjoy long life on the earth" (v. 3).

Could it be, I wondered, that long, fulfilling spiritual life is being withheld from the Church until she honors the origins of her faith? Could it be that our history of division will cease only after we unite with God's chosen family? Marty Waldman thinks so. He believes that the reemergence in our day of the messianic Jewish community is the provision of God to address this great wound of division so that true healing can be brought to the Church.

OUR BLOODSTAINED HANDS

God often requires confession of sin and restitution to be made for the sins of former generations.

Soon after David became king over all Israel, there was a three-year famine. Perplexed over this crisis, "David sought the face of the LORD. The LORD said, 'It is on account of Saul and his blood-stained house; it is because he put the Gibeonites to death'" (2 Sam. 21:1).

Saul? What did Saul, who was now dead, have to do with David? David was not responsible for Saul's sins, was he? And the Gibeonites? That was a reference to a covenant made by Joshua hundreds of years earlier (see Josh. 9). Could that long-ago broken promise be affecting David's reign? Could yesterday's sins really be the cause of today's famine?

Yes! That is exactly what God was telling David.

As Israel entered the land, their leader, Joshua, made a covenant with the Gibeonites. Four hundred years later, Saul, the first king of Israel, broke that covenant. The famine that blighted the land during David's reign came because Saul had dishonored and killed a covenant people. This godless deed, committed centuries later, now rested on the head of the present ruler, and God expected an appropriate act of contrition and confession.

The Church finds herself in a similar place today. Past generations of leaders have dishonored and even killed this special people whom God marked for blessing. We are the descendants, both physically and spiritually, of those generations. Authority has now passed to us just as it did to David. From us as well, the Lord expects humility, acknowledgment of sin and appropriate action before the curse can be removed.

If the spiritual famine of our day is to be stopped, if the "greater riches" revival is to escalate, if this "life from the dead" for God's chosen is to continue, then we must extend hands of petition to a forgiving God, hands of healing to a wounded people.

"Thy kingdom come! Thy will be done on earth as it is in heaven," we have been praying for these hundreds of years. The Church has known its moments of glory as we have traversed the continents to tell the world of its Redeemer. But we have never come into our fullness. Too often our prayers have risen from hate-filled hearts and bloodstained hands.

WELCOME HOME!

The Church is coming to grips with her sins. Reconciliation groups are meeting in every nation. Germans are confessing to Europeans, Japanese to Asians, descendants of European conquerors to indigenous people groups, sons and daughters of former slaveholders and slave traders to sons and daughters of former slaves.

The Jewish issues are no longer being ignored. I am a part of a group that calls itself the Toward Jerusalem Council II. We use the word "toward" because we know we are looking forward to a time when an official church council will be called. We use the words "Jerusalem Council II" because this will be a follow-up of the original council described in Acts 15. In that assembly the Jewish believers met to decide how to welcome Gentiles without requiring that they become Jews. The Toward Jerusalem Council II will be a Gentile council called to decide how to welcome back Jews without requiring that they become Gentiles. Our group wants "to repair and heal the breach between Jewish and Gentile believers in Yeshua, dating from the first centuries of the Church, and to do so primarily through humility, prayer, and repentance."[4]

We have traveled to Spain, to Rome, to Nicea, to Israel. We have visited with key leaders of historic churches as well as leaders in evangelical and charismatic churches. We have stood together in the ruins of Nicea where Gentiles formed a receiving line to welcome our Jewish brothers. It was our attempt to make amends for the fact that they had not been invited to the A.D. 325 and the A.D. 787 councils!

In Spain, in an act of repentance for the decree made in Elvira in A.D. 306—that Christians were not to receive blessings from Jews—Spanish Christians asked our Jewish brothers to bless them and their fields.

For four hours we prayed at the ruins of Yavneh, where Jewish leaders met in the late first century to decide how the faith should continue without the Jerusalem Temple.

From the Mount of Olives we looked out over the city of Jerusalem and prayed again Jesus' prayer for the city. Then we lifted our eyes heavenward to tell Him that we, too, were anticipating the time when a great host of His own nearest of kin would welcome Him back.

As the Church is beginning to welcome the Jewish people back to their ancestral home, a spiritual awakening is also stirring among this Jacob family. Simultaneously, the unity among believers in the Church, across every denominational barrier, is growing. The most rapidly advancing churches are those that are no longer bound by denominational fervor but by devotion to the King. It is happening as the Lord prayed. As brothers and sisters in this huge spiritual family come together, millions more will come to faith. But the family can only come together as we remember our elder brother, the one through whom our Redeemer has been revealed.

All of this will continue as Israel returns to her ancestral home, just as the prophets foretold.

Notes

1. Frank Kaleb Jansen, ed., *Target Earth* (Pasadena, CA: Global Mapping International, 1989), p. 98.
2. *The World Book Encyclopedia,* 1962, s. v. "mutations."
3. Martin J. Waldman, "Reconciliation: A Jewish-Gentile Issue Facing the Church Today" (paper presented to the Network of Christian Ministries, December 1998), p. 9.
4. From the Statement of Purpose, Toward Jerusalem Council II, 1997. Toward Jerusalem Council II is a steering committee of Jewish and Gentile believers who are targeting the time when the entire Gentile Church calls a second council not unlike the council called in Acts 15. This time, however, it would be called to confess the sins of the Gentiles against the Jews and to welcome Jewish believers back into the family of their own Messiah. See appendix D for a statement of repentance.

CHAPTER 8

RETURN TO THE LAND

Who are these that fly along like clouds, like doves to their nests?

ISAIAH 60:8

I will take the Israelites out of the nations where they have gone. I will gather them from all around and bring them back into their own land. I will make them one nation in the land.

EZEKIEL 37:21,22

It must have been a strange sight. We did not look like garden-ers. Yet there we were, about 20 of us, standing on a rather bar-ren hillside outside the city of Jerusalem, spades in one hand, tiny tree seedlings in the other. We set about digging holes in the ground, where we placed the plants then packed the earth tightly around them before giving them a drink. Each tree honored someone we loved. For every tree planted, we paid $10 to the government of Israel.

Suddenly the whole scene struck some of us as hilarious. After paying the price of the tour, we were now paying additional money for the privilege of planting trees—trees that neither we nor the people being honored were likely ever to see again. What a chamber of commerce this Israeli government has! What other nation has ever conceived of such a revenue-producing plan?

But this nation is different; no other can compare. The title deed to their property was signed by the Almighty Himself. Israel was to be considered the "center of the nations" (Ezek. 5:5). In fact, "when the Most High divided to the nations their inheritance, when he separated the sons of Adam, he set the bounds of the people according to the number of the children of Israel" (Deut. 32:8, *KJV*). We may be working on that one for a while, but that's what the Book says!

The psalmist calls Israel "the people close to his [God's] heart" (Ps. 148:14). "To your descendants I give this land," God promised Abraham, then "signed" a covenant of blood (see Gen. 15:1-20). "To you and your descendants I will give all these lands and will confirm the oath I swore to your father Abraham," the Lord later restated to Isaac (Gen. 26:3). And to Jacob, after changing his name to Israel, He said, "The land I gave to Abraham and Isaac I also give to you, and I will give this land to your descendants after you" (35:12).

"This land"? Which land? The Lord was amazingly precise in defining its borders and boundaries: "From the river of Egypt to the great river, the Euphrates," was His word to Abraham (Gen.

15:18). To the conquering Joshua, 400 years later, He further clarified: "Your territory will extend from the desert to Lebanon, the great river, the Euphrates—all the Hittite country—to the Great Sea on the west" (Josh. 1:4).

The extent of God's land promise is shocking for today's readers. How can it ever be possible that Israel will extend all the way to the Euphrates? Can it be that all or parts of Syria, Egypt, Lebanon, Jordan, Iraq and Iran will one day belong to Israel? What horrific upheaval must take place before that can happen? I do not know the answer, but I ask you to remember that one of the theses of this book is that we take the Word literally unless there is reason to interpret it figuratively. And to assume that the land of Israel will be less than the prophetically defined dimensions of Joshua 1:4 is unwise, particularly in light of the expanding borders of the Land just in the past 50 years.[1]

For how long was this land covenant, this deed, to be valid? That stipulation is exact. "For a thousand generations [that's at least 40,000 years], the covenant he made with Abraham, the oath he swore to Isaac. He confirmed it to Jacob . . . an everlasting covenant" (1 Chron. 16:15-17). But what covenant? "I will give the land of Canaan as the portion you will inherit" (16:18).

This phenomenal covenant of land and love carried with it certain conditions. "If you do not carefully follow all the words of this law, . . . you will be uprooted from the land . . . Then the LORD will scatter you among all nations, from one end of the earth to the other" (Deut. 28:58-64). Luke called it being "taken as prisoners to all the nations" (21:24). This would be the penalty for Israel's unfaithfulness.

Jewish history for almost 20 centuries has proven these words true. It all started when the Assyrians conquered the northern kingdom in 721 B.C. The influential leaders were exiled and dispersed, never to return. Jerusalem and the southern kingdom endured for almost 150 years before the Babylonian invasion destroyed both the city and the Temple. After a 70-year exile, some Israelites returned and the Temple was rebuilt. Then the Romans took over rule and destroyed the Temple in A.D. 70. And for nearly 2,000 years there was no nation of Israel.

The desolation of the Land, described by Isaiah, was complete. "The cities lie ruined and without inhabitant, . . . the houses are left deserted and the fields ruined and ravaged" (6:11). The nation of Israel was, as Ezekiel had prophesied, a valley of dry bones (see 37:1,2).

In the Spirit, the prophet Ezekiel saw that valley full of bones come to life. As he was prophesying, the bones came together. A second prophecy called forth the breath. As Ezekiel prophesied, the whole valley came to life and stood to their feet—"a vast army" (37:10).

As mentioned in a previous chapter, Ezekiel's vision has been used repeatedly to describe a dead Church that needs revival. But the prophet was not seeing a Church; he was seeing Israel. Were we to question that interpretation, the Lord does not leave us in doubt. "These bones are the whole house of Israel," the Lord assured Ezekiel. "I will settle [them] in [their] own land" (vv. 11,14).

This risen-from-the-dead nation was no longer to be two nations as it was prior to the Assyrian and Babylonian conquests. "They will never again be two nations or be divided into two kingdoms" (v. 22). Both Jeremiah and Hosea had been given similar revelations. "The house of Judah will join the house of Israel" (Jer. 3:18). "The people of Judah and the people of Israel will be reunited, and they will appoint one leader"

(Hos. 1:11). Thus unified, they will live and work together in harmony.

RETURN OF THE REMNANT

The return of the dispersed people of Israel is to be "from the four quarters of the earth" (Isa. 11:12), not just from the East—from Babylon—as was the return in 516 B.C. Isaiah makes it clear that this is to be a second return and that it will include immigrants from the north, south, east and west. Isaiah even named some of the lands—Egypt, Africa (Cush) and Babylon—but other regions, referred to as "the islands of the sea" (v. 11), were unknown to him at the time of this writing.

Ships would come "bringing [their] sons from afar" (Isa. 60:9). Others would "fly along like clouds, like doves to their nests" (v. 8), a prophetic reference to air traffic that would fill the skies 2,600 years after Isaiah's time! It was to be a greater exodus than the earlier one from Egypt (see Jer. 23:7,8). The north was specifically pointed out as a land from which many immigrants would come. How interesting that today, one out of seven Israelis is Russian. (Moscow is virtually due north of Jerusalem.)

"Expectant mothers and women in labor" (Jer. 31:8) would be among those returning. When the Yemen Jews arrived in 1950, 12 babies had been born in flight, five in the Ethiopian airlift of May 1991.

The wilderness has burst into bloom (see Isa. 35:1,2). Desert fortunes are being restored. Vineyards have been planted on the hills of Samaria (see Jer. 31:5)—what the news media calls the West Bank.

Wealth from other nations is being invested in Israel (see Isa. 60:5). Even our little tree-planting venture that day brought in some of that wealth.

The return would not be without a struggle. "I will say to the north, 'Give them up!' and to the south, 'Do not hold them back.' Bring my sons from afar and my daughters from the ends of the earth" (Isa. 43:6). "I will send for many fishermen . . . and they will catch them. After that I will send for many hunters, and they will hunt them down" (Jer. 16:16).

Even leaving the Diaspora and returning to the Land is to be a time when "cries of fear are heard—terror, not peace" (Jer. 30:5). All these details of amazing accuracy were written by the prophets so many years ago and are fulfilled or being fulfilled in our day!

THE STORY OF ELIEZER URBACH

One son of Israel who encountered great difficulty in returning to Israel is Eliezer Urbach.[2] I met Eliezer while attending a Jewish meeting in New Mexico. I had heard about this man who, with his younger brother, Ernest, fled from his home in Skoczow, Poland, in September of 1939, when German war planes and soldiers stormed that country. To escape capture, Eliezer and Ernest swam across an icy river, hid in forests and avoided Nazi search dogs on their way to the Russian sector. They arrived there, thinking themselves safe under Communism, only to find that Jewish people were also unwanted in Russia. The two brothers were sent off to a Siberian labor camp where Ernest later died.

After years of starvation and deprivation, Eliezer was ultimately released from the Siberian prison so that the state would not have to bury his malnourished body. But his flight to freedom was far from over.

He found his way first to Uzbekistan and then was jailed again in Afghanistan before reaching his hometown. To his horror he discovered that, in his absence, his entire family had been sent to the gas ovens of Auschwitz, just 30 miles from his village.

Hoping to find a way to survive his personal holocaust, Eliezer joined the Russian army but was arrested for smuggling Jewish people to safety. On his way to a court-martial, he escaped to Munich, Germany, and sought refuge with an uncle who lived in that city. There he found neither a safe haven nor a gracious welcome.

Pushing on to Paris in his quest for freedom, Eliezer connected with one of the Jewish committees formed to aid immigrants.[3] With their help and at one point disguised as a British soldier, he ultimately arrived in "Palestine" just in time to fight in the War of Independence of 1948.

As I looked into Eliezer's bearded, weathered face, deeply carved with pain and suffering, I saw the collective grief of multiple thousands who have died at sea, been held captive in detention camps, scaled mountains, swum rivers and endured every imaginable hardship to reach this land of insecure borders and tenuous freedom.

But I saw something else. Peace was etched across his countenance. Love and compassion shone from his eyes. How was this possible? Forced by the hardships of modern Israel's first years—the early '50s—Eliezer went to Brazil. Invited by a kind Gentile to read the New Covenant, he did. There after many brushes with death, he found life. He found both the God and the Messiah of Israel.

THE FIRST ALIYAH

The first *aliyah*—return to the Land—occurred in the late nineteenth century. In 1882, according to the Jewish census records, there were only about 24,000 Jewish residents of "Palestine" living in 17 agricultural colonies. One of the early pioneers was another Eliezer—Eliezer ben-Yehuda—who spent every waking hour pulling together what would become the resurrected Hebrew language. Another early settler was Polish-born David Green who later took the name David ben Gurion and became Israel's first prime minister.

ISRAEL'S RETURN TO THE LAND CAN ONLY BE EXPLAINED AS GOD FULFILLING THE WORDS OF HIS PROPHETS.

But the man who is given credit for the rebirth of the nation was a young secular Jewish Viennese newspaperman named Theodor Herzl. In Paris, in January 1895, he was present at the public humiliation of Captain Alfred Dreyfus, the only Jew on the general staff of the French army, falsely accused of espionage. As Dreyfus was sentenced, the chants of the crowd changed from "Kill the traitor!" to "Kill the Jew!"[4]

Herzl left that city with an urgency to establish a safe place for Jewish people. Two years later he convened the First World Zionist Congress in Basel, Switzerland. At that first meeting a national flag was selected for Israel—the blue and white of the prayer shawl—and a national anthem was chosen, *"Hatikvah,"* meaning "The Hope." An elected Jewish executive was chosen to guide the movement, and a Jewish National Bank and a Land Bank were created with which to begin buying land in the area of the new state.

Perhaps the next really significant piece of the fulfillment of Theodor Herzl's dream came through the work of a Jewish scientist named Chaim Weizman, who had produced a synthetic acetone used in gunpowder needed by the British during World War I. When asked the price of remuneration, he replied, "If Britain wins the battle for Palestine, I ask for a national home for my people in their ancient land."[5]

His request resulted in the Balfour Declaration, issued on November 2, 1917. "His Majesty's Government views with favour the establishment in Palestine of a national home for the Jewish people, and will use their best endeavour to facilitate the achievement of this object."[6]

Later in the same month, the British general Sir Edmund Allenby led the charge that gave Great Britain control over Jerusalem. As he was entering the city through the Jaffa Gate, he dismounted his horse and took off his hat, believing that none but the Messiah should enter Jerusalem mounted on a steed.

This intriguing story is reminiscent of many of the battles of Israel in earlier years. General Allenby had ordered planes to fly overhead and leaflets to be dropped, calling the Turks to surrender. These leaflets, signed by Allenby, were taken by the Turkish Muslims to be a directive from Allah for them to leave the city. Not a shot was fired. Ramon Bennett describes the event in his book *When Day and Night Cease,* and refers to Isaiah's prophecy: "Like birds flying about, so will the LORD of hosts defend Jerusalem. Defending, He will also deliver it; passing over, He will preserve it" (Isa. 31:5, *NKJV*).[7]

Following World War I, in 1920, the League of Nations gave Britain control of "Palestine," but the Balfour Declaration had been forgotten. Fear of Arab reprisals turned British hearts against the Jewish immigrants. Refugees were not allowed to land in the Haifa harbor, and the quota of returning Jews was greatly reduced. Britain installed an Arab government over much of the land that had been biblically promised to Israel.

Another war and a lifetime of horror would transpire before the world's conscience was sufficiently pricked to establish that homeland for the Jews promised by His Majesty. The British government had long since washed its hands of the whole affair. Illegal immigrants were sent back to their city of origin or held in detention camps in nearby Cyprus. The fate of the potential Jewish nation now rested in the hands of the United Nations.

A NEW NATION

The United Nations began to consider the partitioning of "Palestine" to create a homeland for the Jews. A two-thirds majority of the nations was necessary in order for the State to be established.

In the two months leading up to the decision, the Bible College at Wales, under Rees Howells's leadership, concentrated 11 days of prayer on the United Nations vote. "I firmly believe the time of the Gentiles is drawing to a close, and the Jews must be back in their own land when the Master comes," Rees had said.[8]

On the evening of November 24, 1947, the college received word that the partitioning had not carried. The intercessors prayed more fervently and saw in faith "God's angels influencing those men in the United Nations conference in New York to work on behalf of God's people." When news came the following day that the petition had passed, the college called it "one of the greatest days for the Holy Ghost in the history of these 2,000 years."[9]

President Harry Truman's support was essential if the vote was to pass, but he was slow in adding his weight. In fact, the president had been ignoring all requests for a meeting about the partitioning until leaders from the Jewish community contacted Truman's good friend and former business partner, a Jewish man named Eddie Jacobson. Jacobson appealed to the president's sense of history and prevailed upon him to meet with Chaim Weizman, who, though in very poor health, had traveled to the United States and was waiting in a hotel room until the appointment could be secured.

It was this visit with Weizman, the hero of Britain's win in World War I, that strongly influenced Truman's ultimate decision. Without that encounter, the resolution would not have passed. With the president's pressure on several key countries, the vote was taken: 33 nations voted in favor, 13 against, with 10 abstentions. The date was November 29, 1947.[10]

Herzl had spoken prophetically when, in 1897, he predicted that within 50 years the State of Israel would be birthed. Isaiah's words of 2,700 years earlier had become a reality (see Isa. 66:8). A country was born in a day!

NONE LEFT BEHIND

In spite of the vote, the young nation had to battle seven Arab nations—Egypt, Jordan, Lebanon, Syria, Saudi Arabia, Yemen and Iraq—to establish itself. Reading about those days is like reading a page from the books of the Kings or Chronicles in the Bible:

Israel fielded 18,000 men, 10,000 rifles, 3,600 sub-machine guns, a few old field guns, two tanks, and four planes, of which two were shot down the first day.

Israel was not only hopelessly outnumbered, she did not even possess sufficient guns for each man to have one of his own! Against full-fledged air forces, Israel had next to no air power. And if they had not somehow stolen two tanks from the British, they would have been completely without armour. Nevertheless, by the time the UN managed to arrange a cease-fire between the warring parties, Israel was holding nearly three times the area of land that she had been allocated in the partition![11]

Every Israeli war has seen its miracles. There was a time in the 1967 Sinai campaign when two Israeli tanks topped a sand dune and found themselves facing a complete Egyptian tank unit. With no explanation, the Egyptians stopped, opened their turrets, jumped out and began to flee through the desert. After the Egyptians were captured, they explained their actions, telling stories of the "hundreds of Israeli tanks" they had encountered.[12]

During the 1973 Yom Kippur war, Syria marched across the unprotected Golan Heights. They could have been in the city of Haifa within 24 hours had they not suddenly stopped on the ridge of the Jordan River, nearly within firing range of the city of Tiberias, and remained there for three days. This gave the Israelis time to muster their forces and engage the Syrians in battle. Why did the Syrians remain on the ridge? A nonreligious Israeli general described a "great gray-white hand pressing down onto the Syrians from out of the sky."[13]

Israel's return to the Land can only be explained as God fulfilling the words of His prophets. At a time when there seemed to be no way for them to go on, the Lord provided a way.

Many of the wars initiated against Israel only ended with an increase in square miles for the fledgling nation. When the new

State of Israel was established, the landmass consisted of 3,000 square miles. At the conclusion of the War of Independence in 1948, that had increased to 8,000 square miles. The Six Day War of 1967 expanded her landmass to 26,000 square miles; the Yom Kippur War of 1973, to 36,000 square miles, though some of this has now been returned. But even this did not yet measure up to Israel's full inheritance as promised to both Abraham and Joshua (see Gen. 15:18; Josh. 1:4).

At the time the State of Israel was formed, Israel's population was less than 1 million. By 1973, it was still less than 3 million. Today the total population has reached 6 million, of which approximately 5 million are Jewish. In the 50 years of Israel's history, her people have returned from over 100 nations and have endured six wars.

But the story is not complete. There are still 12 million, perhaps more, of Israel's children scattered throughout the nations. Ezekiel speaks of a time when they will all gather to their own land, "not leaving any behind" (Ezek. 39:28). If the prophet's words are to be taken literally—and this is always the assumption until proven otherwise—then every Jew will one day return to the land of Israel.

Similarly, if Paul's words are to be taken literally—and why not?—all Israel will be saved. Does this mean every single Jewish person? Let us believe so and pray and move toward that end.

Notes

1. Israel was granted a certain land allotment for the State in the United Nations resolution of November 1947. The surrounding Arab nations did not honor that resolution, however, and went to war immediately upon the declaration of the State of Israel in May 1998. A few days later those same Arab nations were calling for a cease-fire, with Israel gaining additional land in this war they had neither initiated nor desired. A similar thing happened in the Six Day War of June 1967. Shortly after war was

declared, Syria, one of the chief aggressors, seeing that Israel was within firing range of her capital city of Damascus, sued for quick resolution. Egypt, in the same war, basically lost her complete air force in the early days of fighting. At the end of the war, Israel's landmass was several times larger than at the outset of the war. The Yom Kippur War of 1973 was no different, though Israel was less prepared for battle. Nevertheless, in every war with her neighbors, Israel's boundaries have increased. If she had not given back land for peace, she would today be many times larger than required by the original UN resolution.

2. For a complete account of Eliezer Urbach's story, see his book *Out of the Fury: The Incredible Odyssey of Eliezer Urbach* (Charlotte, NC: Chosen People Ministries, 1987).

3. The Hebrew Immigrant Aid Society is affiliated with Jewish committees in the United States.

4. Larry Collins and Dominique Lapierre, *O Jerusalem! Day by Day and Minute by Minute, The Historic Struggle for Jerusalem and the Birth of Israel* (New York: Simon and Schuster, 1972). The story of Dreyfus, Herzl and the Jewish nation is well told in this volume.

5. Ramon Bennett, *When Day and Night Cease* (Jerusalem: Arm of Salvation Press, 1992), p. 92.

6. Tom Hess, *Let My People Go! The Struggle of the Jewish People to Return to Israel,* 5th ed. (Charlotte, NC: MorningStar Publications, 1997), p. 174.

7. Bennett, *When Day and Night Cease,* p. 92.

8. Norman Grubb, *Rees Howells, Intercessor* (Fort Washington, PA: Christian Literature Crusade, 1952), pp. 229, 230.

9. Ibid., p. 224

8. Collins and Lapierre, *O Jerusalem!,* pp. 187-190.

10. Bennett, *When Day and Night Cease,* p. 164.

11. Ibid., p. 165.

12. Ibid.

13. Ibid.

CHAPTER 9

THE AWAKENING

They will come trembling to the LORD and to his
blessings in the last days.

HOSEA 3:5

I did not know their names. In fact, I had never met any of them.
Yet, while driving through the streets of Jerusalem one day, I
prophesied over the people as I passed by. The car windows were
rolled up so that none could hear me, but that was not important. I was foreseeing a time when many of these people would
come to know Yeshua as Messiah. I have read their Scriptures
that speak of Israel's awakening when they are back in the Land.

Later, I stood before a Jewish congregation in Haifa. Behind me was the ark that contained the Torah scroll, the handwritten words of Moses that are read in the synagogues of the world each Sabbath. Before me were 150 believers in Yeshua, living evidence that the words of Isaiah are being fulfilled in our day.

"It is a joy to see you with my natural eyes," I said. "For years I have seen you with my spiritual eyes. I have read about you in the words of the prophets and the apostles. But now you are here. More of you are coming. I see tens of thousands of family members and friends who will come to faith in the Messiah Yeshua. Who of you would have imagined 10 years ago that today you would believe that Yeshua/Jesus is the Messiah of Israel? But the Lord has drawn you. This is the day for your eyes to be opened."[1]

REUVEN'S STORY

Reuven Doron is the grandson of early twentieth-century Russian immigrants to Israel. On foot, one of his grandfathers crossed the mountains of Turkey and eventually wound up in northern Galilee. The other brought his family by ship. Both played significant roles in the founding of the young nation.

At age 19, Reuven served in a specialized military unit on the Golan Heights in the Yom Kippur War of 1973. Two-thirds of the men in his unit never made it home. Though Reuven survived the war, he was left with questions for which he had no answers. He was restless, disillusioned and grieved. What was life all about? What meaning could there be to the tragedies he had experienced?

He packed his bags and headed out into the world—Europe, Canada and Central America—before settling in at the Business

College of Arizona State University in Phoenix. There he had a life-defining encounter with the God of Israel.

In order to help finance his schooling, Reuven gave private Hebrew lessons. One of his students was a Gentile named Frank. "Why would you, a blond, blue-eyed Gentile, want to learn Hebrew?" Reuven asked him one day.

"Because I've always wanted to be able to read the Scriptures in the original Hebrew language," the man replied. "In the Bible I find the knowledge of the living God."

Reuven never recovered from this candid answer. He had studied the Bible in the schools of Israel, but for him it was merely a book of ancient legends and national myths. God was distant, impersonal and uninvolved with daily life. Now Reuven had to take another look. Could it be that this Book did reveal the living God?

"If there is a God, if He is at all interested in me, if He really paid for my sins, then not only do I want to read about Him and hear of Him, I need to know Him!" Reuven admitted to his student.

"Then go pray. Seek His face," was the advice given.

Reuven accepted the challenge. Night after night he poured out his questions to this faceless God who did not seem to answer.

Yet he knew that one question remained, a question that no Jewish man or woman wants to ask. Could it be that this One whom Christians have worshiped through the ages, this Jewish man whose followers sometimes turned against Israel—could it be that He was the Promised One?

Reuven felt trapped by his own need to know truth. Finally, frustrated and angry, he hurled his one remaining question into the night sky. "Do I need Him? Do I need the Nazarene in order to come to You?"

Let Reuven tell you in his own words what happened next.

This time, God answered! Out of heaven came an arrow of revelation, piercing through the darkness of the night, through the world and through my soul. His Word now sparked my spirit alive with a blaze of truth as He spoke, "Yes" and "Amen! You need the Nazarene!"

For the first time in my life, I consciously heard God. The ring of His Word was so clear and loud that, even if the word had come audibly, the sound would have been insignificant compared to the thunder in my spirit! And so I stayed right there, kneeling in my backyard, drinking in the life and nectar of His Word. . . . It was some time before I stood to my feet and returned to my apartment. To my amazement, a most unusual sensation and realization came upon me. I remember saying to myself, "Reuven, you have changed. You need to get reacquainted with yourself." You see, though I had no intellectual knowledge of the new birth doctrine, I simply was spiritually "born again" as the seed of heaven was planted in my heart![2]

Hosea had spoken of Reuven and a host of other Jewish believers living in our time.

The Israelites will live many days without king or prince, without sacrifice or sacred stones, without ephod or idol. Afterward the Israelites will return and seek the LORD their God and David their king. They will come trembling to the LORD and to his blessings in the last days (Hos. 3:4,5).

No king or prince since 586 B.C., when Nebuchadnezzar took Zedekiah to Babylon (see Jer. 52:9-11). No sacrifice since the forces of General Titus destroyed the Temple in A.D. 70. Our day is the "afterward" in which Reuven and hundreds of thousands of other sons and daughters of Jacob have come or will come trembling to the Lord and to His blessings in these last days.

ISAIAH'S MANDATE

Isaiah, too—who had a terrifying encounter with the Holy One, the God of Israel—had foreseen the day in which we live. He heard the angels worshiping around the throne. He felt the doorposts and thresholds of the Temple shake. The air was filled with smoke. Isaiah cried, "I am ruined! For I am a man of unclean lips . . . and my eyes have seen the King, the LORD Almighty" (Isa. 6:5).

An angel came and touched his mouth with live coals from the altar, saying, "Your guilt is taken away and your sin atoned for" (v. 7).

Then the Lord spoke, "Whom shall I send? And who will go for us?" (v. 8).

"Here am I. Send me," Isaiah blurted out, having no idea of the message he was to deliver to Israel (v. 8).

"Go and tell this people," the Lord said. " 'Be ever hearing, but never understanding; be ever seeing, but never perceiving.' Make the heart of this people calloused; make their ears dull and close their eyes. Otherwise they might see with their eyes, hear with their ears, understand with their hearts, and turn and be healed" (vv. 9,10).

Jesus used Isaiah's words to explain why Israel as a nation did not receive Him (see Matt. 13:14,15). The apostle John also remembered Isaiah's prophecy when he said, "Even after Jesus had done all these miraculous signs in their presence, they still would not believe in him" (12:37). Indeed, John says, "They could not believe" (John 12:39). "God gave them a spirit of stupor," adds the apostle Paul, referring back to the same words of Isaiah (Rom. 11:8).

"Could not believe"? "Spirit of stupor"? Those are strong terms.

What does this mean? The ways of the Lord are beyond our comprehension. Why would God close Israel's corporate eyes and ears to the very message they were destined to bring to a lost world?

"Because of their transgression, salvation has come to the Gentiles," Paul continues in the same Roman letter (Rom. 11:11).

Could there have been no other way? Paul is silent. God is silent.

"Their transgression means riches for the world, and their loss means riches for the Gentiles" (v. 12).

"Unfair!" we cry. But there is no answer. Only the testimony of the centuries that Isaiah heard accurately.

HOW LONG?

Isaiah's revelation did not stop with closed eyes and ears and a hardened heart. For how long, O Lord? he asked. How long will this last? How long will their eyes be closed? How long will their hearts be hardened?

Isaiah had spoken of deserted homes, ruined fields and a forsaken land—words that were fulfilled in detailed accuracy. The Babylonians, Persians, Greeks, Romans, Byzantines, Arabs, Turks, Crusaders and British—each ruled the land before another "Israel" arose.

During those intervening centuries, fields were salted to destroy their fertility. Trees were cut down to avoid the taxation levied against them. Malaria swamps became commonplace.

When Mark Twain visited Israel during the latter part of the nineteenth century, he described it as a land that was utterly desolate. Yet the Jewish people have always been drawn back to this promised inheritance. Through the ages their Passover liturgy—"Next year in Jerusalem!"—has reminded them of their ultimate homeland.

"As the terebinth and oak leave stumps when they are cut down, so the holy seed will be the stump in the land," Isaiah was told (Isa. 6:13).

The stump would grow again. Israel would return. And when she returned, Isaiah's "until" would be fulfilled: Her eyes and ears would not remain closed, her heart no longer hardened.

Ezekiel's valley of dry bones vision (see Ezek. 37) parallels Isaiah's vision. Isaiah saw the land devastated, the population gone; Ezekiel saw a valley of dry bones, a nation that no longer existed. Isaiah saw a stump that would grow again; Ezekiel saw the bones come together—the northern and southern kingdoms united, no longer two nations, but one. He saw breath—spiritual life—entering the resurrected nation.

I will take you out of the nations; I will gather you from all the countries and bring you back into your own land. I will put my Spirit in you and move you to follow my decrees and be careful to keep my laws. *Then [you] will know* that I am the LORD (Ezek. 36:24,27,38, italics added).

You will know that I am the Lord when the fields are again plowed and sown! You will know that I am the Lord when I multiply your population again! You will know that I am the Lord when the towns are inhabited and the ruins rebuilt! You will know that I am the Lord when the number of men and animals dwelling in you increase! You will know that I am the Lord when I make you more prosperous than before!

THE JESUS GENERATION

The year 1967 is a date to remember.

Since the first century, there has never been a generation that has seen so many Jewish people in so many parts of the world—both in Israel and in the Diaspora—coming to believe in Jesus. Something happened in the heavens when Jerusalem came under Israeli control in 1967.

SINCE THE FIRST CENTURY, THERE HAS NEVER BEEN A GENERATION THAT HAS SEEN SO MANY JEWISH PEOPLE IN SO MANY PARTS OF THE WORLD COMING TO BELIEVE IN JESUS.

The June 21, 1971 issue of *Time* magazine carried an extensive article describing the Jesus Movement of the late '60s. Three times in the article, the writer dates the beginning of the movement to 1967.[3] It was during that era that a great majority of today's leaders in the messianic Jewish movement came to faith in Yeshua.

Joseph Shulam, a native Israeli messianic leader in Jerusalem, says,

> In the early 1960s, it was difficult to find even two dozen Jews in Jerusalem who believed in Yeshua the Messiah. Those who were around lived under a terrible fear of being exposed and totally ostracized by the Jewish community. Now, fifty years later, there are hundreds, if not thousands, of Jews in Jerusalem who believe that Yeshua is the Messiah and participate in one of the nine Hebrew-speaking congregations which meet in Jerusalem. If the L-rd would grant us in the next fifty years the same kind of growth in the Body of the Messiah as we had in the last fifty years, we will have a Messianic Jew as the president of the State of Israel![4]

Joel Chernoff, general secretary of the Messianic Jewish Alliance of America, agrees. "Messianic Judaism is by far the fastest growing stream of faith within the Jewish community."[5]

Isaiah's vision is coming to pass. Eyes are opening, sometimes almost involuntarily. Most would prefer that their search for truth *not* end in Jesus. Yet they *do* want truth.

———

I met Gari when she moved to Nashville from Florida. Her faith in Jesus came after being partially paralyzed for eight and a half years following an automobile accident. Reared in New York, she had gone to the beach, crutches and all, for a time of rehabilitation. A "beach evangelist" began a conversation with her.

"I'm Jewish," she had told him. "We do not believe in Jesus." And yet something in her began to stir. Why was she so annoyed? Did this unexpected encounter touch a need within her?

Later she hobbled into a restaurant and found the only vacant stool at the bar. The man sitting next to her began to dialogue. He told her that he often frequented bars to find people who were in need of an eternal answer to their problems—the answer was Jesus!

After giving her usual "Not interested" reply, she found herself accepting his invitation to attend a church. She was later irritated by her own unaccustomed response, but she was not one to go back on her word.

When she sat down in the church, she could not help but notice the jacket worn by the man beside her. It was a denim jacket with a huge star of David on the back. Inside the star was a Christian symbol. She wept during the entire two-hour assembly.

What is this? she wondered. *Am I being brainwashed? What is happening to my emotions? I'm out of control!*

Back at her mother's home, Gari opened up some of the literature given to her at the church. Among the pamphlets was a brochure telling how to accept the Lord, and it included a sample prayer for inviting Jesus into one's heart. As Gari read the words, she started to pray and then stopped abruptly, astonished at her own reaction. Then, almost carelessly, she added, "Jesus, if You are real, I need to know it."

The bones in her spine began to crack as the long-time paralysis lifted from her body. Even an astigmatism in her eyes, which she had had all her life, was healed!

For 15 minutes she paced the floor in wonder, believing herself to have been caught up in some kind of dream. She did not want to leave the room for fear it was all in her imagination.

"You *are* real!" she finally declared to the Messiah she had never known.

Gari loves to tell the story. Now she is praying for that sovereign intervention of God in the lives of her family and friends.

———————

Stan Telchin, a Million-Dollar Round Table insurance man, was trying to convince his older daughter that her newfound faith in Yeshua was invalid when he came to faith. He bought Bibles, commentaries and study guides and set out to prove that Jesus is not the Messiah. He went to his rabbi with his questions, looking for a reason not to believe. Stan was so emotionally opposed to his own findings that he could not admit his faith. Not until he heard himself ending a prayer in the name of Yeshua was he aware that faith had arisen in his heart without his conscious permission. His spiritual eyes were opened, just as Isaiah had said they would be!

Stan's wife, Ethel, had a similar experience. "I had gone to bed the night before, still believing that while Jesus was a good man, He was not who He said He was. When I awoke in the morning, I knew it was true. *Jesus is the Messiah.*"[6]

———————

Faith came to Dr. Stephen Stracher, a flight surgeon with the Federal Aviation Administration, while in a Zen meditation hall. He had been told that Jesus and Buddha were saying the same thing, yet he could not harmonize Jesus' agony on the cross with Buddha's relaxation enlightenment.

Pondering the paths of Jesus and Buddha, Stephen realized that, in order to understand how these two paths merged, he would have to experience Jesus fully. But how? Remembering Jesus' claim to be the Messiah of Israel, he knew the answer. To experience Jesus, he must accept Him for who He says He is.

Stephen says, "I said loudly in my mind with complete conviction, *Jesus, I accept you as the Messiah of Israel.* In my mind I heard the words, *The Passover Lamb who takes away the sin of the world.* Without warning or preparation . . . to my utter astonishment I suddenly saw that it was true!"[7]

The revelation of Jesus as Messiah came to Dr. Vera Schlamm while reading from the prophet Isaiah. Vera and her family were freed from the Bergen-Belsen concentration camp following the Allied victory in February 1945. Becoming a believer in Jesus was the last thing she intended to do, but she was on a serious search for God and was reading from a Bible someone had given her.

"When I came to [Isaiah] 53," she says, "it seemed so obvious that it was talking about Jesus that I thought, *Well, this is a Christian translation, and they have slanted the text to sound that way.* So the following Friday night at the Temple Emmanuel, which I attended regularly, I took the Scriptures from the pew and opened to chapter 53 of Isaiah. The wording was a little different—but it *still* sounded like Jesus!" Only a short time later, Vera confessed her faith in Him.[8]

Much of the Church in this generation has been surprised by the escalation in the numbers of Israel's children coming to faith. Others have been expecting it.

Some of our Jewish representatives from the Toward Jerusalem Council II Committee met recently with two prominent theologians in the Eastern Orthodox Church. After introducing themselves and explaining their mission—to challenge the Church to receive them—our representatives heard the learned men say, "We knew, from our own study of Scripture, that you would be coming. We just did not know that you were already here!"

Do you understand now why I was so confidently praying over my nameless friends in the streets of Jerusalem? Why I know that many of them will yet come to believe? Can you also comprehend why my heart vibrates with joy with each new account of a child of Israel who has come home? Why the prophets' words keep resounding in my Spirit?

Centuries ago, long before any of these believers were even born, Hosea, Isaiah, Ezekiel and Paul were seeing Reuven, Gari, Stan and Ethel, Vera, Stephen and thousands more—eyes open, ears listening, hearts softening—receive their King.

Notes

1. In a subequent visit only six months later, there were 200 believers in this Jewish congregation!
2. Reuven Doron, *One New Man* (Cedar Rapids, IA: Embrace Israel, 1996), p. 47.
3. "The New Rebel Cry: Jesus Is Coming!" *Time* (June 21, 1971), p. 59.
4. "The Theology of Israel's Fiftieth Birthday," *Teaching from Zion* (Jerusalem: Netivyah Bible Instruction Ministry, 1998), p. 2.
5. Joel Chernoff, "The Lord Is Gathering His People," *Charisma* (April 1997), p. 53.
6. Read Stan and Ethel's complete story in his book *Betrayed* (Old Tappan, NJ: Chosen Books, Fleming H. Revell, 1981).
7. Dr. Stracher's story is told in the book *Jewish Doctors Meet the Great Physician,* Ruth Rose, ed. (San Francisco: Purple Pomegranate Productions, 1998), pp. 55-68.
8. Ibid., pp. 107-122.

CHAPTER 10

THE RESURRECTED "NAZARENES"

I am a Jew.

ACTS 22:3

Not since the demise of the Nazarene communities of the third and fourth centuries have so many of Israel's children come to faith in Yeshua. Jewish believers in those intervening years had been convinced by the Church to give up their own God-given ordinances and feasts to embrace Gentile Christian practices. Those practices were sometimes a coating of Christianity over former pagan customs. The winter equinox celebration, with its trees and Yule log that honored Nordic gods, was translated into Christ Mass, the celebration of the birth of Jesus. Passover became Easter. Circumcision, not required of Gentiles, was replaced by infant baptism and christening. Bar Mitzvah was now confirmation. The Jewish expression of faith in the Jewish Messiah was lost.

This all began to change in 1882, with an influential Jewish leader from Kishinev, Maldova, named Joseph Rabinowitz. Reared in a rabbinical household, Rabinowitz had been ensnared by the skepticism of the Enlightenment. In the face of growing persecution of the Jews in Russia, Rabinowitz had gone to Palestine to consider setting up a colony of returning immigrants. While there, he had a life-changing encounter with the Messiah on the Mount of Olives and went back to his homeland convinced that "Jesus is the King, the Messiah, who alone can save Israel!"[1]

Three years later, in January 1885, the first assemblies of the Israelites of the New Covenant were held. Throngs of people gathered—some out of curiosity, some out of interest, others to cause disturbance. At one point, police officers were posted at the door to keep order. In early February of that year, a street demonstration broke out, threatening Rabinowitz with violence.

All of this did not deter him. In 1890, with the permission of the Russian authorities, Rabinowitz opened the first messianic synagogue in modern history. Jacob Wechsler, a contemporary of Rabinowitz and a translator of some of his sermons, said, "Who would have believed before that around 100 Israelite men would each Sabbath assemble in a house built in honour of Jesus the Messiah?"[2]

After his Mount of Olives experience, Rabinowitz was absorbed with two subjects—Israel and Yeshua (he always used

Jesus' Hebrew name), and he refused to relinquish his Jewish identity. Until his death in 1899, his passport proclaimed him a Jew. On his tombstone, at his express wish, were inscribed these words: "An Israelite who believed in Jehovah and His Anointed, Yeshua of Nazareth, the King of the Jews, Joseph, son of David, Rabinowitz."[3]

SIGNS OF THINGS TO COME

The insistence that he was still Jewish, even though a believer in Yeshua, brought Rabinowitz into continual conflict with both the Church and the Jewish community. Just as in the case of the earlier "Nazarenes," much of the Church did not know what to do with him, and the Jewish community considered him a traitor to the faith of his fathers.

Rabinowitz was very clear in his belief that "through faith alone in Yeshua the Messiah all men may be justified without the works of the law." Yet he insisted that since "we are the seed of Abraham according to the flesh . . . we are bound to circumcise every male child on the eighth day, as God commanded. And as we are the descendants of those whom the Lord brought out of the land of Egypt with a stretched out arm, we are bound to keep the Sabbath, the feast of unleavened bread, and the feast of weeks, according as it is written in the Law of Moses."[4]

Although the Church as a whole was not comfortable with his unorthodox views, some welcomed Rabinowitz as a first-fruits fulfillment of end-time prophecy. A number of mission boards, influenced by the earlier Puritans' revelation about the Jewish people, were also ready to receive him. Franz Delitzsch, professor of Old Testament at Leipzig, translator of the New

Testament into Hebrew and himself a Hebrew Christian, befriended Rabinowitz, as did Alfred Edersheim, the highly respected Jewish Christian theologian.

The synagogue in Kishinev would have been a strange combination for either Jew or non-Jew. Everyone sat bareheaded, and yet there was a menorah. An ark at the front of the hall contained the Torah scroll. The Sabbath text was taken from the portion of Torah for that particular Sabbath, as was the custom in a synagogue. Rabinowitz would often kiss the Torah scroll in Jewish fashion, yet the Gospels would also be read.[5]

Support for the new synagogue began arriving from the London Mildmay Mission in England, from the Danish Israel Mission, from churches in Glasgow and Edinburgh, the Swedish Mission and mission groups in Germany. Rabinowitz began to receive more invitations than he could accept. In 1893, he spent over a month in the United States and was invited by Dwight L. Moody, the well-known evangelist, to preach to a Jewish audience at the World Exposition in Chicago.

Rabinowitz was careful to position himself outside of denominational affiliation. He considered the rebirth of the Jewish believing synagogues a resurrection of the early Jewish community, a regrafting of Jewish branches, and felt that this awakening of Israel to faith in their Messiah would "impart the highest life to the dead world," an obvious reference to Romans 11:15.[6]

Peter Hocken, the contemporary Roman Catholic priest and author, recognizes this same need. In his book *The Glory and the Shame,* Hocken writes:

It is of vital importance for the proper contribution of Messianic Judaism to Christian unity that Gentile

Christians, whether Catholic or Protestant, give them the space to develop in fidelity to the Spirit and to make their unique contribution to Catholic-Protestant reconciliation.[7]

In other words, it is important that Jewish believers in Jesus be allowed to find their way to biblically orthodox faith, within a modern Jewish expression.

Kai Kjaer-Hansen, Rabinowitz's biographer, sums up the man's life with these words: "The lasting significance of Rabinowitz's activity lies first and foremost in his stubborn insistence that his faith in Jesus had not made him an ex-Jew, and that his Jewish identity had not been drowned in baptism."[8]

Rabinowitz himself compared the Jewish situation to a doctor and his patient. When the doctor is diagnosing the patient's illness, he presses various places on the body, asking such questions as, "Does that hurt? Is this sore? Is there pressure here?" Only when the doctor touches the diseased part of the body does the patient wince in pain.

As long as Rabinowitz spoke disparagingly of the Tanakh, no one flinched. He could even maintain that the writings of Moses were only the writings of a man, not the revelation of God, and the Jewish community was silent. He might even deny God without stirrings. But when he returned to the Holy Land, speaking of Yeshua as the Messiah, he heard screams of pain from all sides.

In spite of the excitement of Jewish mission agencies around the world, Rabinowitz's reestablished Jesus-believing synagogue in Maldova had no permanence. The Russian government's permission for the strange Jewish house of worship was granted only to Rabinowitz personally and died with him. There was no successor. The chapel closed after his death, opening for a brief period before becoming a Greek church and then a cinema. It would appear to be the end of an era.

THE LEGACY OF JOSEPH RABINOWITZ

Yet the memory of Joseph Rabinowitz lingered, fueling the flames of a growing interest in Israel and the Jewish people. Remember that these were also the years of Theodor Herzl and the Zionist movement, the time when both governments and churches were awakening to a possible rebirth of the Land.

The Hebrew Christian Alliance of America was formed in 1915 "to bring together Jewish believers for fellowship and to be a light to their people."[9] Jewish people began coming to a saving knowledge of Yeshua as Messiah and Savior and joining the mainstream churches in major cities of the United States and England.

In July 1928, the International Hebrew Christian Alliance met in Hamburg, Germany. Sir Leon Levison, the president of the Alliance, mentioned Rabinowitz in his address to the conference. In the summer of 1931, S. H. Wilkinson visited Kishinev and read from the Hebrew Bible which had been in Rabbi Rabinowitz's possession.

In London, the Mildmay Mission to the Jews that had supported Rabinowitz, established a Hebrew Christian congregation. Other such congregations began to spring up with the intention of keeping many of the biblical customs while holding the line that salvation is altogether by grace through faith.

But these were not synagogues such as Rabinowitz had begun. These were missions witnessing to the Jewish people about their

Jewish Messiah with the assumption that those who received Him would be a part of an established church.

This was still the thinking at the time of Martin Chernoff's acceptance of his Jewish Messiah in 1940. His wife, Yohanna, tells the story in her book *Born a Jew... Die a Jew.*[10] Marty became an ardent disciple of the Lord, sharing his faith passionately with both Jew and Gentile but assuming that all would join "the Church." For the next 30 years he worked in Jewish missions in the framework of an existing church. Although there were several such Jewish missions, Marty and Yohanna were surprised at the number of Christians who did not believe that a widespread revival was possible until after the rise of the Antichrist and the rapture of the Church. These Christians were not prepared for the unexpected developments of the next few years.

MESSIANIC JUDAISM IS BORN

And then the year that brought a change in the heavenlies. In the late spring of 1967, five surrounding Arab nations began to move their armies and war machinery to Israel's border, intending to destroy the nation. On June 5, Israel launched its pre-emptive strike and routed those nations in the now-famous Six Day War. At war's end, Jerusalem, including the Western Wall, the Temple Mount and much of Judea (now "Palestinian" territory) and Samaria (the West Bank) were under Israeli control.

About the same time, there began to be a noticeable increase of Jewish believers in Jesus. In the United States, many of those came through the Jesus Movement that had its beginning in 1967. The need to disciple many of these ardent young believers pushed the Chernoffs toward a major shift in perspective.

The Hebrew Christian Alliance of America conference took place just a few days after the close of the war. There the Chernoffs sensed change in the air. They were filled with excitement. The retaking of Jerusalem was obviously another sign from heaven and they were eager to hear what the prophetic teachers and theologians would say.

They found only confusion. Neither Jewish nor Gentile believers knew how to interpret the recent news, and not one conference speaker made reference to it. Martin and Yohanna did not know that many of these scholars had been teaching that Jerusalem would not be back in Israeli control until after the return of the Messiah. They were silent because they had not had time to rearrange their theology!

For the next few years, Marty and Johanna struggled to hear the heart of God for their young flock. These Jewish believers, like Rabinowitz 100 years earlier, found no cause to relinquish their Jewishness. They, like the early believers in Acts, were Jews who wanted to worship in Jewish synagogues as followers of Yeshua. There was no such option available.

In early 1970, Marty Chernoff received a visionary directive from the Lord. Two words were emblazoned across the sky in the form of a banner: *Messianic Judaism*. Marty understood that to mean that the time had come to form a body of believers that was not bound to the format of the Church. It was time to open a Jewish synagogue of believers in Jesus.

In October of that year, the Chernoffs resigned from their missions board and incorporated Congregation Beth Messiah in Cincinnati, Ohio. Later they moved to Philadelphia and assumed the leadership of another messianic congregation, Beth Yeshua, continuing their relationship with the Hebrew Christian Alliance. In 1975, the name was changed to the Messianic Jewish

Alliance of America, with Beth Yeshua as one of the visionary congregations on the forefront of the movement. There are now about 80 congregations affiliated with the MJAA.

Historian David Rausch says, "The name change . . . signified far more than a semantical expression—it represented an evolution in the thought processes and religious and philosophical outlook toward a more fervent expression of Jewish identity."[11]

There were similar stirrings in other Jewish hearts. Marty Waldman described his own feelings about being a Jew in a Gentile church when he came to faith in the mid-'70s:

> Although I was generally welcomed into the Church, I soon discovered that my desire to remain identifiably Jewish in my faith was not only discouraged, but oftentimes brought confusion and even accusations of "judaizing." As a new Jewish follower of Jesus, I was experiencing an identity crisis that would not go away.[12]

Today Marty is the spiritual leader of Baruch HaShem, a messianic synagogue in Dallas, Texas.

Daniel Juster, who came to faith in a Dutch Reformed church and was ordained in a Presbyterian church, began to be drawn back into his own Jewishness and became the founding president of the Union of Messianic Jewish Congregations in the late '70s. Another 80 or so congregations have membership in the UMJC. Juster would later help to begin the *Tikkun* (restoration) network that oversees congregations in the United States, with covenant partners in Israel and the former Soviet Union.[13]

The International Federation of Messianic Congregations is a smaller group that is working and praying toward a Sephardic revival through Yeshua. This organization oversees a number of congregations in the United States as well as in Central and South America.

None of this existed before 1967, the year the Lord turned that prophetic key in the heavens to unlock some of the hearts of His covenant people.

FALL OF COMMUNISM— RISE OF EVANGELISM

Messianic Judaism of the 1980s necessarily concerned itself with developing a full-orbed Jewish expression of faith in Yeshua. Weddings, Bar Mitzvahs, day schools, yeshivot to train messianic rabbis—all emerged. Yet one vital element of the original first-century messianic community was still lacking—apostolic outreach.

In the early '90s, after the fall of Communism, an amazing spiritual hunger surfaced in Eastern Europe and it became a ripe field for harvest. Enter Jonathan Bernis, executive director of Hear O Israel Ministries. Bernis gained a vision for taking the gospel to these Eastern European children of Israel, many of whom had forsaken their Jewish identity after generations of persecution and the atheistic indoctrination of Communism. His organization began sponsoring Jewish cultural festivals, always honoring Holocaust survivors, many of whom have received the Messiah. "Since our first festival in '93," he reports, "over 125,000 Russian Jews have made professions of faith in Messiah, and more than a dozen Messianic Jewish congregations have been planted and are thriving there."[14]

Today messianic congregations are also flourishing in Canada, Western Europe, South America, New Zealand and Australia. These congregations bring together Jews and Gentiles in their common faith. Churches in Asia and Africa are awakening to God's irrevocable call on Israel and are restoring Jewish roots. According to one of my friends who has spent his life among the Arabs, even among these sons of Ishmael there is a growing recognition that "salvation is from the Jews" (John 4:22).

Joseph Shulam reports of nine Hebrew-speaking congregations in Jerusalem. Reports from the rest of Israel are encouraging, even though not yet spectacular. Some congregations number as many as 250 members. Others consist of only a few people meeting in a home. A recent survey, conducted by Kai Kjaer-Hansen and Bodil F. Skjott and published in Jerusalem, lists 81 congregations and house groups now meeting throughout Israel.[15]

IN JESUS-BELIEVING SYNAGOGUES THERE ARE NOT ONLY JEWISH BELIEVERS BUT THERE ARE A NUMBER OF COVENANT GENTILE PARTNERS WHO ARE CONNECTING TO THEIR OWN JEWISH ROOTS— A FORESHADOWING OF THE FUTURE.

In 1967, there were no messianic Jewish congregations in the world. Today, according to an article in *Christianity Today*, there are over 350.[16] In 1967, there were an estimated 2,000 believers in Jesus among the Jewish people. An article in *Charisma* magazine mentions a 1990 survey that suggests that more than 1 million Jewish people in the United States alone express "some sort of faith in Yeshua."[17]

It is no longer unusual to meet Jewish people who have accepted Jesus as Messiah. Many of these believers are still a part of the Church in its non-Jewish expression. Some have remained in their local synagogues. That is changing as more and more Jesus-believing synagogues are forming. In these synagogues there are not only Jewish believers, but there are also a number of covenant Gentile partners who affirm God's call to Israel and are connecting to their own Jewish roots—a foreshadowing of the future.

GROWTH IN THE MIDST OF OPPOSITION

This new profile is emerging despite sometimes fierce opposition. During the early days of Philadelphia's Beth Yeshua, there were bomb threats and death threats. Tires were punctured. Children were spat upon. The Jewish community was irate that a messianic synagogue was about to buy property in their community. Billboards warned of this "cult" in "your neighborhood" and of the need to "guard your children."[18]

A parade of protest was planned for a Sunday morning. Busloads of participants arrived from other cities. Members of Beth Yeshua turned the intended threat into a celebration of Jewish music and dance and a proclamation of the Jewish Messiah.

Not long ago in Dallas, Texas, the Baruch HaShem congregation was gathering for the Sabbath morning worship when a machine-gun-wielding neo-Nazi invaded their quiet surroundings. The fact that no one was killed can be credited only to the Lord. Twice the man aimed his gun and pulled the trigger, only to have the gun mysteriously raised to fire harmlessly into the empty skies. Mothers and children froze in fear; some were wounded as they crawled through windows to escape the shooting spree before police arrived and subdued the man. He was later convicted and is spending several years behind bars.

In the former Soviet bloc, the opposition has also been fierce. One messianic Jewish festival and conference had to be canceled because the police could not assure protection for those attending. At other events, large halls were emptied mid-performance because of repeated bomb threats.

Resistance is increasing in Israel as well. Returning believing immigrants have been denied citizenship on the basis of their faith. *Sabra*—native-born Israelis—and other believers have been beaten. Houses and synagogues have been vandalized. In one incident the congregation was surrounded while the Sabbath worship was in progress. The worshipers could not leave until police protection was secured.

This scenario is looking more and more like the early centuries, but the "Nazarenes" are back—this time to stay!

A NEW THING

As these synagogues are formed, there have been many questions. The Rabinowitz model is over 100 years old, and Rabinowitz himself did not have all the answers.

What part of Jewish heritage should be maintained and what part relinquished? What should be incorporated into the new synagogues? What expressions of Jewishness are valid, and which run at cross-purposes to newly acquired faith?

Should there be a Torah scroll? Should the congregations read weekly from those scrolls? Should the meetings be held on the Sabbath? What kind of worship music should be used? Should dance be introduced into worship? Should men wear a *yarmulke*—a small head covering? A *tallith*—Jewish prayer shawl? What form of government? Should the synagogue leaders be called rabbis? How much, if any, Jewish liturgy?

How much should be received from the (Gentile) Church without giving up Jewish identity? What should be done about Gentiles who want to join the movement? Should they be considered for leadership? What can be done to maintain Jewish identity if Gentiles do join? How can Jews unite with the Gentile Church and yet remain Jewish?

Dan Juster, in his book *Jewish Roots,* writes:

Sometimes Messianic Jews, in seeking to recapture their Jewish roots, become enamored of Rabbinic customs and Rabbinic worship. I have become convinced that Rabbinic Judaism is a more severe departure from biblical faith than I had ever realized in my early days of Jewish recovery. . . . The atmosphere of the New Testament carried on the spirit of the Hebrew Scriptures pervasively and profoundly. The essence of Rabbinism is a severe departure, replacing revelation with human reason. . . . We who are Jewish are biblical New Covenant Jews, not Rabbinic Jews![19]

Juster believes that this newly resurrected community is to encourage more creatively produced materials that reflect the fullness of faith in the context of Jewish life and usage. These areas include Jewish dance, food, Hanukkah celebrations, Purim plays, Bar and Bat Mitzvahs (the celebration of young manhood at age 13; young womanhood, often at 12), marrying under a *chupah*—the canopy used for the bridal party during the wedding ceremony—all valid expressions of Yeshua-affirming, Torah-honoring Jewish faith. Torah and Haftorah reading—readings from the Prophets and the historical books—on the Sabbath also keep the connection to the larger Jewish community.

There is not always agreement on the answers to these questions. For several years the UMJC (Union of Messianic Congregations) and the MJAA (Messianic Jewish Alliance of America) were largely estranged from each other. But as maturity and grace increased, these movements have reconciled and today are enjoying renewed fellowship.

The Church, too, continues to assess this resurrected community. Rick Joyner, author and publisher of *Morning Star Journal*, wrote that he was at first disturbed by the determination of some in the messianic movement to maintain some degree of separateness from the Church. Later he began to believe that distancing had been essential.

> As it has been widely taught, there are three basic levels to relationships. The first level is codependence. The next level is independence. The final, and highest, level of relationship for which we need to strive, is interdependence.
>
> On the level of codependence, the weaker personality is usually swallowed up in the stronger one. Because of this, a person usually must go through the phase of independence when they find their identity and become secure in it before they can go to the highest level—interdependence. For this reason the Messianic movement needed to remain independent from the Church until its identity was established. Its identity must be strong enough for a relationship with the Church in which it will not be swallowed.[20]

The return of so many Jewish people to the Messiah in our day reaffirms God's covenant love for His people. We are living out the fulfillment of Isaiah's vision when Jewish eyes would open. We are experiencing what Hosea predicted—Israel coming "trembling to the LORD" (Hos. 3:5). We are watching the breath blown into the resurrected body of which Ezekiel spoke. Paul's words concerning the regrafting are taking on more weight. And we are pondering anew the words of Jesus from that day overlooking the Temple, "When these things begin to take place . . . your redemption is drawing near" (Luke 21:28).

The Lord refuses to close the curtain of history without His beloved Israel.

Notes

1. Kai Kjaer-Hansen, *Joseph Rabinowitz and the Messianic Movement: The Herzl of Jewish Christianity* (Grand Rapids, MI: Wm. B. Eerdmans, 1995), p. 19
2. Ibid., p. 74.
3. Ibid., p. 70.
4. Ibid., p. 104.
5. Ibid., pp. 151, 152.
6. Ibid., p. 5.
7. Peter Hocken, *The Glory and the Shame: Reflections on the 20th Century Outpouring of the Holy Spirit* (Guildford, England: Eagle, 1994), p. 160.
8. Kjaer-Hansen, *Joseph Rabinowitz and the Messianic Movement*, p. 233.
9. The founding of the Hebrew Christian Alliance in 1915 is mentioned in Michael Schiffman, *Return of the Remnant—The Rebirth of Messianic Judaism* (Baltimore, MD: Lederer Messianic Publishers, 1992), p. 27.
10. For the complete story of the Chernoffs, see Yohanna Chernoff, *Born a Jew . . . Die a Jew: The Story of Martin Chernoff, a Pioneer in Messianic Judaism* (Hagerstown, MD: EBED Publications, 1996).
11. David Rausch, quoted in Chernoff, *Born a Jew . . . Die a Jew*, p. 178.
12. Martin J. Waldman, "Reconciliation: A Jewish-Gentile Issue Facing the Church Today," (unpublished), p. 2.
13. See Appendix C for further information about *Tikkun*.

14. Jonathan Bernis, "Have You Hugged a (Messianic) Jew Lately?" *Charisma* (April 1997), p. 68.

15. Kai Kjaer-Hansen and Bodil F. Skjott, *Facts & Myths About the Messianic Congregations in Israel* (Jerusalem: United Christian Council in Israel in cooperation with the Caspari Center for Biblical and Jewish Studies, 1999), p. 16.

16. Gary Thomas, "The Return of the Jewish Church," *Christianity Today* (September 1998), p. 63.

17. Thomas, "The Lord Is Gathering His People," *Charisma* (April 1997), p. 54.

18. Chernoff, *Born a Jew...Die a Jew,* pp. 183-197.

19. Dan Juster, introduction to *Jewish Roots: A Foundation of Biblical Theology* (Shippensburg, PA: Destiny Image Publishers, 1995).

20. Rick Joyner, "The Messianic Movement," *Morning Star Journal,* vol. 10 (Charlotte, NC: MorningStar Publications, 1999), p. 42.

JEW AND GENTILE— "ONE NEW MAN"

His purpose was to create in himself one new man out of the two.

EPHESIANS 2:13

"I'm confused! Is Yeshua not a Jewish Messiah? Is this not my own heritage? Shouldn't the Church be affirming their Jewish roots rather than requiring me to become more like a non-Jew? Is it wrong for me to want the Church to understand?"

In a home gathering of Jewish and Gentile believers, these questions were voiced by a woman who had recently moved to our city from Israel. She was having difficulty finding her place among the community of believers.

I remembered the story of David and Martha Stern, a Jewish couple who are part of a messianic congregation in Jerusalem. In a conversation with the pastor of a large American church, the pastor spoke of a messianic leader whom he greatly admired. "But why does he have to be so Jewish?" he exclaimed. To which Martha Stern responded reflexively, "Why do *you* have to be so Gentile?"

The Church has become a Gentile-Moabitish expression of faith in the Messiah. Still, we consider our churches to be culturally neutral and wonder why Jewish believers would not feel welcome among us, not knowing how far removed we are from the family that birthed us. When we read Paul's Ephesian letter and hear him speaking of Jew and Gentile as "one new man" (2:15), we assume that this one new man will look like regular church with Jewish believers added to the mix. Jewish believers, on the other hand, often wonder how the Church can be so insensitive.

HONORING JEWISH HERITAGE

Even though there was no requirement made of the early Gentile believers to become Jewish, it was necessary for them to learn of their Jewish roots and heritage in order to understand faith in Messiah. New Testament Scripture can only truly be understood when overlaid by the Hebrew Scriptures—the Old Testament, the Torah and the Prophets. These early Gentile believers had only these Jewish Scriptures and were therefore being taught the Tanakh—the Hebrew Scriptures. Only gradually did the new writings of the apostles gain in authority.

The entire New Testament, much of it written for a Gentile audience, is rooted in the Tanakh. Jesus is the Suffering Servant and the Lamb of God. Jewish genealogy is the heritage of both Jew and Gentile. The Genesis account, the Flood, the tower of Babel, the call of Abraham, the sacrifice of Isaac, the Israelites' deliverance from Egypt and, led by Moses, the establishment of the kingdom of Israel—these events form the backdrop from which all history is perceived.

This early "one new man" of which Paul spoke was the coming together of Torah-observant Jewish believers in Yeshua with Gentiles, who though never required to keep the Law, were nonetheless becoming well grounded in *their* Jewish past.

Paul's Roman letter, written to the most pagan city of the day, constantly refers to both Jews and Gentiles as he works to establish the faith of these former pagans—now believers in the one true God of Israel and in Israel's Messiah.

Three times Paul mentions that the gospel application was "first for the Jew" (Rom. 1:16; 2:9,10). Paul himself was specially called to Gentiles, yet he reminds his Roman hearers that he still has "great sorrow and unceasing anguish" in his heart, because of Israel's rejection of their King (9:2). "Theirs is the adoption as sons; theirs the divine glory, the covenants, the receiving of the Law, the temple worship and the promises," he mourns (9:4), even as he assures his non-Jewish readers that they, too, have now been accepted into the family of faith. As far as salvation is concerned, "there is no difference between Jew and Gentile" (10:12), he says, but calling and gifting are another matter. Israel's call is irrevocable (see 11:29).

Paul speaks often of the Law, though these former pagans had never been to synagogues where the Torah was read each Sabbath.

Another of Paul's letters is written to Ephesus, known as the city of the "temple of the great goddess Artemis" (Acts 19:27). Paul reminds the Ephesian believers that in former times they were "separate from [Messiah], excluded from citizenship in Israel" (Eph. 2:12). Now they were "no longer foreigners and aliens, but fellow citizens with God's people" (2:19). They were "heirs together with Israel" (3:6).

Fellow citizens with God's people? Heirs together with Israel? The very thought must have been offensive to some of his readers, but that did not deter Paul. His Ephesian readers "once were far away" but had been "brought near through the blood of [Messiah]" (Eph. 2:13). They were reconciled to God and to each other, where both have "access to the Father by one Spirit" (v. 18).

Ruth (the Gentiles) has not replaced Boaz (the Jewish people), only joined him—become a member of his family, a citizen of his land and partaker of his promises. She has come from a land of famine and been welcomed into the house of abundance. She is now an heir together with Boaz, not an heir in place of him. She was at one time a foreigner to the covenants of the promise that were his; now she is a sharer together with those promises. She must be careful to "no longer live as the Gentiles do" (Eph. 4:17).

In the Ephesian letter there is a certain implied knowledge of the Hebrew Scriptures. This knowledge was resident in these former Artemis worshipers because of Paul's earlier visit to the city, a visit that lasted over two years (see Acts 19:1-20).

The Jerusalem Council (see Acts 15) had made it plain that circumcision and the feasts, kosher living and the Sabbath were not binding on the Gentiles. Paul addresses these issues with both the Romans (see Rom. 14:1-8) and the Colossians (see Col. 2:16,17). Yet some of these early Gentile converts celebrated the feasts. This was true in pagan Corinth, where Paul warned the people about the manner in which they were observing Passover (see 1 Cor. 5:7). We do know with certainty that Gentiles will one day (in the millennial kingdom?) celebrate the feasts (see Zech. 14:16,17).

For that matter, could it be wrong for me, a Gentile, to celebrate Passover on the Jewish calendar, remembering my own deliverance from death as well as the deliverance of the family who brought me life? Would the Lord be displeased with me, a covenant member of the family by adoption, if I choose to use this time to teach my children and grandchildren about this God who always keeps His promises and who is one day coming to deliver us in another grand exodus from this planet of slavery to bring us into our promised inheritance?

Why should I not choose to build a *sukkah* on my back porch during the Feast of Tabernacles? Why not seize this time with my children and grandchildren as an opportunity to teach them of the temporary nature of our existence, of Jesus who tabernacled among us, of the provisions "our" people experienced in the 40 years of wandering?

What better time to speak of the coming of the Holy Spirit than the annual day of remembrance on God's calendar of *Sukkoth*, 50 days after the Crucifixion day at *Pesach*? What riches are there for Gentiles who observe these special feast days, depicting our mutual heritage of faith?

RETURN TO UNITY

In those early congregations, Jew and Gentile lived together in love and unity. True, there is "neither Jew nor Greek," as Paul told the Galatians (Gal. 3:28), yet that does not eradicate their distinctiveness. (Male and female are also "one in [Messiah]," Paul said at the same time, but who would ever question the uniqueness of each?)

The fact that salvation comes through the Jews—that it is to be preached "first to the Jew"—need not be an affront to any people. Israel's surrounding Arab nations, for example, who have found it difficult to acknowledge her identity, will only enter their intended destiny as they recognize Israel's Messiah and her claim to the Land deeded to her by God. Ezekiel spoke specifically about a time when "aliens"—those who are not descendants of the 12 sons of Jacob—will be considered "native-born Israelites," in line for an inheritance along with the tribes of Israel (see Ezek. 47:22) but only as they honor, even join, this chosen family of God.

Isaiah foresees a time when non-Jews will be appointed as priests and Levites (see Isa. 66:18-21). Non-Jews enter their full inheritance only as they recognize and submit to the Jewish Messiah.

For a brief moment in history, there existed a fascinating blend of Jew and Gentile as Jewish apostles preached the good news to the nations in the early first century. That unique blend began to be marred as Gentiles kept Jewish Scripture but renounced much of their Jewish legacy. Their oneness was further damaged when the Church began to demand that Jewish believers forsake their own God-ordained, fulfilled-in-Messiah customs and feasts and join in the often rooted-in-paganism Gentile culture. Jesus' reference to "the times of the Gentiles" was now understandable.

THE TIMES OF THE GENTILES

Both Jesus and Paul imply that Gentile dominance would end: Jesus spoke of the "times of the Gentiles" being fulfilled (Luke 21:24); Paul said "the full number of the Gentiles" would "come in" before the change would occur (Rom. 11:25). Paul obviously did not mean there would be no more Gentiles coming to faith, since he had just referred to the great revival that would break out when Israel began to receive Messiah (see v. 12). What did Paul mean? To what did Jesus refer?

The history of Israel, from the call of Abraham to the baptism of Cornelius, had been the "times of the Jews." Although there were occasions when God revealed Himself to people other than Abraham and his sons of the promise, the most consistent and clearest revelations were reserved for this covenant family. Only they were given prophetic insights into man's future redemption through a messiah.

WE ARE ABOUT TO SEE JEWISH LEADERSHIP RESTORED TO THE ENTIRE BODY OF THE LORD.

Cornelius's miraculous welcome into this otherwise Jewish family began a rapid transition. Within a few years, the leadership had changed, and for the next 19 centuries we entered into the "times of the Gentiles." Amazingly, Jewish tradition speaks of 2,000 years before Torah, 2,000 years of Torah and 2,000 years of the Gentiles. Then the Messiah is to come and usher in a "sabbatical" seventh millennium.

Today the scene is changing again. Israel is back, and that great revival is encircling the globe, just as Paul foretold. Gentiles are repenting of centuries-long anti-Semitism and again recovering

Jewish roots. A love for Jewish people is being sovereignly poured into the hearts of the Gentile Church. "Ten men from all languages and nations will take firm hold of one Jew by the hem of his robe" and say [both literally and figuratively] 'Let us go with you, because we have heard that God is with you'" (Zech. 8:23).

We are about to see Jewish leadership restored to the entire Body of the Lord. We are entering a time when the Jewish nation will become known as worshipers of Jesus/Yeshua, and the whole Church will honor and accept Israel's fulfilled role as a light to the nations (see Isa. 60:3). If that statement seems far-fetched, consider that the events of the last 50 years would have been deemed impossible a generation ago!

It could be a combined Jew/Gentile leadership that we are to expect. First, in the time of the Jews, the leadership was Jewish. Then came the time of the Gentiles. But we will see the coming together of a Jew/Gentile Bride before the Lord's return.

The transition from Jewish to Gentile leadership required several decades. The transition to a Jew/Gentile leadership is still in its initial stages, and we cannot be sure what form it will take. One thing is certain: Jewish believers are here to stay. Another is equally certain: Jewish leadership in the whole Body of the Lord is rising again. Furthermore, Jerusalem, Israel and the Jewish people are moving again into the prophecy-fulfilling stage of world history.

FUTURE ROLE OF JERUSALEM AND ISRAEL

It was to Israel and Israel's Messiah that God said through Isaiah: "Arise, shine, for your light has come. Nations will come to your light" (Isa. 60:1,3). That prophecy was only partially fulfilled in earlier centuries. Israel's full destiny has yet to be realized. An international revival of praise and righteousness is still ahead (see Isa. 61:11). Sometime in the future the nations of the world will participate in the annual Feast of Tabernacles (see Zech. 14:16). God's calendar of New Moons and Sabbaths will take on renewed meaning for all mankind (see Isa. 66:23). Jesus Himself will eat the Passover in the fulfilled kingdom of God (see Luke 22:16).

Jerusalem, Zion and Israel will be the esteemed names of an honored people, as former oppressors bow at their feet, calling them "the City of the LORD, Zion of the Holy One of Israel" (Isa. 60:14). Jerusalem will be a "crown of splendor in the LORD's hand" (Isa. 62:3). This is why Isaiah will not remain silent until he sees righteousness shining out and salvation blazing forth from this favored city (see Isa. 60:1,2).

With the prophet Isaiah, we yearn for that time when the knowledge of the Lord fills the earth like waters cover the sea (see Isa. 11:9), when all Israel will be righteous and possess the land forever (see Isa. 60:21).

With Jeremiah, we agree that "Judah will be saved and Jerusalem will live in safety" (Jer. 33:16).

We pray and we wait. We wait for His [Messiah's] feet to "stand on the Mount of Olives," for the mountain to be "split in two" (there is a geological fault line at just the right place) and for the Lord to reign as "king over the whole earth" (Zech. 14:4,5,9).

We look for the time when children live out their intended life spans; when wolf and lamb, lion and calf, lie down together; when "the infant will play near the hole of the cobra," and there will be neither harm nor destruction "on all my holy mountain" (see Isa. 11:6-9; 65:20,25).

We pray, we wait and we hope.

"Lord, are you at this time going to restore the kingdom to Israel?" the disciples inquired following Jesus' resurrection and shortly before His ascension (Acts 1:6).

"It is not for you to know the times or dates the Father has set by his own authority," was Jesus' reply (v. 7). In other words, "You have accurately read the Prophets. There will be a restoration of the kingdom to Israel. Your thinking is correct, but the timing is not for you to know."

Jesus must remain in heaven until time for everything to be restored "as he promised long ago through his holy prophets," Peter told his listeners a few days later (Acts 3:21).

How do we act in this interim as we await the ultimate fulfillment? What does this "one new man" look like in these early days of the twenty-first century?

We will see a return to that which was begun in the first century. Jewish believers remain Jewish in practice, often in their own synagogues, as Gentile congregations are restored to an appreciation of their Jewish heritage.

As we revive that first-century model, more and more messianic Jewish synagogues will arise. Gentiles will choose to be a part of those congregations as they grow in love for the Jewish people and reclaim their lost Jewish roots. Daily Bible readers will refrain from mentally substituting the word "Church" when reading "Israel" and will receive God's heart of compassion for His Covenant people and their role in world redemption. The biblical calendar will take on new significance as the redeemed from all nations will see the imprint of God in these fulfilled and being-fulfilled-in-Messiah annual reminders. These Gentile believers will delight in joining their Jewish brothers and sisters in proclaiming God through the biblical feasts. They will want to express their love for the God of Abraham, Isaac and Jacob in practices He ordained.

At the same time, the heart of the Church will begin to be turned in love for Jerusalem, for Israel and for all Jewish people everywhere. Mission efforts around the world will begin to remember Paul's "first-to-the-Jew" admonitions to the Romans. Pastors who are preaching in an expository way through the book of Romans, will no longer ignore chapters 9 through 11 as if they were an interruption in an otherwise excellent epistle. Church choirs will be rehearsing their Christmas specials and begin to weep as new revelation opens their hearts to the literal meaning of the words they are singing:

O come, O come, Emmanuel, and ransom captive Israel!
Rejoice, rejoice, Emmanuel will come to you, O Israel![1]

Note
1. John Mason Neal, *"Psalteriolum Cantionum Catholicarum."* The words of this Latin hymn, composed in 1710, were written in 1851.

CHAPTER 12

A TIME TO PRAY

*You who call on the LORD, give yourselves no rest, and give him no rest
till he establishes Jerusalem and makes her the praise of the earth.*

ISAIAH 62:6,7

The year is 522 B.C. Daniel, having lived in Babylon for almost as
long as he can remember, is now an old man. One day, while
reading from the Jeremiah scroll, he is held captive by the
prophet's clear prediction: "When seventy years are completed
for Babylon, I will . . . bring you back to this place" (Jer. 29:10).

It's true, Daniel thought, as he remembered the years since
his own deportation to Babylon under Nebuchadnezzar. Five

other kings reigned in Babylon before its fall to Persia. Then a new king by the name of Cyrus ascended Persia's throne.

Anticipation was high among the exiles in Babylon when Cyrus became king. Isaiah had called this man by name almost two centuries before his birth, predicting that he would issue a decree to free the exiles and begin the rebuilding of the city and the Temple (see Isa. 44:28 and 45:13). It happened exactly as Isaiah had foreseen that Cyrus would decree: "Let [Jerusalem] be rebuilt . . . Let [the Temple's] foundations be laid" (cf. Ezra 5:13).

The work on the city and the Temple began with great exuberance. But King Cyrus died before the work was completed, and Persia's next king was not so favorably disposed toward these sons of Israel.

It is the first year of king Darius's reign as Daniel is again reading the familiar words. "Seventy years," he muses as he reads from Jeremiah. "It has been 70 years since the Temple was destroyed. The full number of the years is fast approaching. The fullness of the time has come. *HaShem's* (Hebrew for "The Name") Word never fails. We must continue in prayer until we see its completion."

Daniel lays aside the scroll and begins to pray:

O Lord, the great and awesome God, who keeps his covenant of love with all who love him and obey his commands, we have sinned and done wrong. We have been wicked and have rebelled; we have turned away from your commands and laws. We have not listened to your servants the prophets. . . .

Lord, you are righteous, but this day we are covered with shame . . . because of our unfaithfulness to you. O

Lord, we and our kings, our princes and our fathers are covered with shame because we have sinned against you. . . .

Now, our God, hear the prayers and petitions of your servant. . . . O Lord, hear and act! For your sake, O my God, do not delay (Dan. 9:4-19).

As Daniel knelt in prayer, he was carrying upon his shoulders the sins of generations—from Judah and all Israel, those in the land and those in exile, kings and princes. He confessed sins for which he was not personally responsible but whose tragic consequences had shaped his life.

King Darius needs to read this, Daniel may have thought. *He needs to know that his own grandfather Cyrus was named as Israel's benefactor over 200 years ago. He needs to see Jeremiah's prediction of the return.*

The scene is imagined, but the facts are true. It was in the first year of Cyrus's reign that Jeremiah's prophecy began to be fulfilled (see Ezra 1:1). It was in the sixth year of Darius's reign when the Temple was completed (see 6:15).

By that time, Ezra and Nehemiah had returned to Jerusalem with "Daniel prayers" on their own lips. "O my God, I am too ashamed and disgraced to lift up my face to you . . . our sins are higher than our heads. . . . From the days of our forefathers until now, our guilt has been great," Ezra agonizes as he intercedes before God (9:6,7).

"I confess the sins we Israelites, including myself and my father's house, have committed against you. We have acted very wickedly toward you," Nehemiah laments (Neh. 1:6,7), as this civil governor agrees with the prayers of Ezra the priest.

PARTNERS WITH GOD

From the reading of Scripture as well as interpreting the times, Daniel, Ezra and Nehemiah knew of God's intentions for their day. They also understood that they could partner with the Lord to help bring about its completion. Daniel's partnership was primarily in prayer and fasting (see Dan. 9:2,3). Ezra and Nehemiah, who returned to the Land, led the people in repentance and in the rebuilding of the wall.

WE HAVE SEEN A PARTIAL FULFILLMENT OF GOD'S
WILL REGARDING ISRAEL, HER COMING TO FAITH
AND THE WORLD REVIVAL. OUR ROLE IS TO GIVE
OURSELVES TO INTERCESSION, CONFESSING THE
SINS OF OUR FATHERS AND RULERS UNTIL WE SEE
THE WORK COMPLETED.

Our position today is precisely the same as Daniel's in his day. We have seen a partial fulfillment of God's will regarding Israel, her coming to faith and the world revival. Our role, like Daniel's, is to give ourselves to intercession, confessing the sins of our fathers and rulers until we see the work completed.

God is looking for those who will join Him in His work. "I looked for a man among them who would . . . stand before me in the gap on behalf of the land," He told Ezekiel (22:30). "Whatever you bind on earth will be bound in heaven," Jesus told His disciples, obviously not to affirm their selfish desires but in order to release His plans upon the earth. "If two of you on earth agree about anything you ask for, it will be done" (Matt. 18:18,19).

In John's vision of heaven, the work of God could not be released upon the earth until the bowls of incense, containing the prayers of the saints, were filled (see Rev. 5:8; 8:3-5). Paul assures us that the promises of God will all be fulfilled. Yet the "Amen" is to be spoken by us (see 2 Cor. 1:20).

Strange. There are plans of God that will not go into effect until we first pray to know His will and then pray for it to be done. It is out of this understanding that Isaiah cried, "Give yourselves no rest, and give him no rest till he establishes Jerusalem and makes her the praise of the earth" (62:6,7).

Daniel read Jeremiah and would not rest until he saw the fulfillment of what he had read. Ezra and Nehemiah understood the intentions of the Lord in their day and could not rest until it was accomplished.

I am a Daniel! I am an Ezra! I am a Nehemiah!

I am Don! I have seen the sins of my people! They are mine to confess and mine to renounce. It is my role to intercede, to stand in the gap, to ask for mercy for us all. I understand some of the Lord's intentions for our day and will not be quiet until they happen.

I have read Jeremiah. I have listened to Isaiah. Words from Hosea and Zechariah and Ezekiel pulsate within me. I cannot rest, will not rest, do not want to rest until I see with my own eyes what the Lord has spoken!

That is the reason why I and others, Jew and Gentile together, traveled to Spain to pray in the room where Ferdinand and Isabella signed the decree to evict the Jews from Spain and confiscate their wealth. We wanted to confess the sins of our people and to ask the Lord to cover our sins with His blood. We wanted to pray that the Lord would restore us to each other.

That is why we sat in the dust together in shame and grief after seeing the chains on the wall of the San Juan de los Reyes cathedral in Toledo, Spain.

That is why we Gentiles formed a reception line for our Jewish brothers and sisters when we visited the ruins of Nicea. These brothers had not been invited to the earlier councils, and we were grieving their loss and exclusion.

That is why some of us who are non-Jews went to the annual meetings of the Messianic Jewish Alliance of America and the Union of Messianic Jewish Congregations and knelt before the entire assembly to confess our own sins and the sins of generations preceding us. We love our Jewish family and we want to be with them!

Have mercy on us, Lord! Change our hearts! O Lord, listen! O Lord, forgive! O Lord, hear and act! For Your sake, O my God, do not delay!

Lord, raise up Daniels, Ezras and Nehemiahs in our day, men who will see what You have intended and who will stay before You until the vision is accomplished. Raise up the Ruths and Rahabs who will experience Your presence, who will covenant with You and with Your people to usher in Your work.

The psalmist said, "If I forget you, O Jerusalem, may my right hand forget its skill. May my tongue cling to the roof of my mouth if I do not remember you, if I do not consider Jerusalem my highest joy" (Ps. 137:5,6)!

CHAPTER 13

THE FINAL EXODUS

They overcame him by the blood of the Lamb and by the word of their
testimony; they did not love their lives so much as to shrink from death.

REVELATION 12:11

For almost 400 years, Israel had languished in Goshen. Father
Jacob's assurance that they would be rescued from this foreign
land was a vague dream. Then one day things began to happen.
There were rumblings that an exit was imminent—reports of
miracles. These reports were often confusing, since Pharaoh's
magicians were also producing "signs." Then other marvels—a
series of plagues that not even the court sorcerers could mimic.

The faithful God-followers in the area of Goshen were marvelously protected from the plagues but faced the fury of the incensed taskmasters of Egypt.

The last plague was released on Passover night. The blood of a slain lamb, painted on the doorposts, was the sign of obedience necessary to protect Israel's firstborn sons. Death reigned in Egypt that night, from the house of Pharaoh even to the livestock in the fields. Wails of grief could be heard throughout the land. In Goshen, the Israelites were quietly sequestered behind bloodstained doors. Not even a dog barked to disturb the peace (see Exod. 11:7).

The yearned-for moment had arrived. At midnight the call went forth. Israel was released from her centuries-old slavery. God was calling her home.

One final hurdle lay ahead—the crossing of the Red Sea. According to every visible assessment, defeat seemed sure. Hemmed in by the approaching chariots of Pharoah in swift pursuit behind them, and the deep waters in front of them, there was no escape. But the Lord fought for Israel that night. The waters of the sea divided and a pillar of fire lighted the exit route for the 2 million Israelites leaving Egypt.

Today we stand poised for another great exodus. It has not been 400 but 2,000 years since Yeshua said to His disciples, "I will come back and take you to be with me" (John 14:3).

For two millennia the family of Messiah has languished in a foreign country, waiting for His return. Today there are rumblings that another exodus is imminent. The signposts to which he pointed—the events that would take place before His return—are appearing.

Three significant, predicted signs indicate that the day is near. Israel's second exodus from the nations to the land of her inheritance is in progress. Jewish people are recognizing their Messiah. The world is in its all-time grand revival of faith in the one true God and His promised Messiah. The day when the skies will part to welcome His return is fast approaching. Luke and Zechariah agree that He will return to the Mount of Olives (see Zech. 14:4; Acts 1:11). John and Isaiah describe an earthly reign of peace (see Isa. 65:18-25; Rev. 20:1-6). In His first advent, Jesus was the Suffering Servant. This time He will come as conquering king.

MODERN-DAY PLAGUES

In spite of growing anticipation of our exodus and the Lord's return, there are difficult days ahead. Jesus spoke not only of uneasy times surrounding Jerusalem's destruction, but also of global labor pangs preceding His arrival.

We can expect a proliferation of miracle-working messiahs and prophets (see Mark 13:22). Wars and rivalry between nations (*ethnos*, "ethnic groups") will increase (see Matt. 24:6,7). Famines and earthquakes will multiply. Wickedness will mature alongside world revival and apostasy (vv. 12-14). "Distress, unequaled from the beginning of the world until now—and never to be equaled again" (v. 21) will descend upon a Church waiting to be delivered. If it were possible (which, thanks be to God, it is not for those who look to Him), even the people of God would be deceived (v. 24).

Paul speaks of the anti-messiah, the end-time Pharaoh, the personification of evil—Satan's own personal representative—who will unite the world against God's people for one last battle before the exodus (see 2 Thess. 2:8-12). Daniel saw that the saints will be "handed over to him for a time" (see Dan. 7:25) and that only those faithful to God will be able to resist him (see Dan. 11:32). Zechariah speaks of a time when the whole world will come with Pharaoh-force against Israel (and those who are covenanted with her); in that moment the Lord will ensure her safety (see Zech. 12:3; 14:2,3).

"But, wait!" you may be saying. "I thought we would be gone before then! Is not the Church to be raptured before this last great tribulation?"

Some believe we will. Others point to the scriptural indications that we must endure the coming "plagues" before our departure.

An interesting Greek word, *thlipsis*, often translated "tribulation" in our English Bibles, gives weight to this understanding. The word can also be translated "anguish, affliction, sufferings, persecution, trouble, hardship, distress, oppression," or even "pressure and stress." Fifty times this word is used in the apostolic writings, often to warn believers that they are not exempt from difficult times.

"Be careful that you do not fall away because of trouble (*thlipsis*) or persecution," Jesus warned (Matt. 13:21, author's paraphrase). In fact, "In this world you will have trouble (*thlipsis*). But take heart! I have overcome the world" (John 16:33).

Paul picked up the theme of enduring many hardships (*thlipsis*) to enter the kingdom (see Acts 14:22), and encouraging believers to be "patient in affliction" (*thlipsis*) (Rom. 12:12). Believe it or not, we are to "rejoice in our sufferings" (*thlipsis*) (5:3).

When Jesus was speaking of end times, He told the apostles that the sign of the Son of Man will appear, the shofar (trumpet) will sound and the Lord will gather His elect "immediately after the distress (*thlipsis*) of those days" (Matt. 24:29). John, in his vision, saw a great multitude from every nation, tribe, people and language standing before the throne. "These are they *who have come out of the great tribulation (thlipsis)*," one of the elders told John (Rev. 7:14, italics added). One has to have been in the great tribulation before he can come out of it.

I could be wrong, but I would rather be prepared for the worst and be delivered than to be caught off guard. Come to think of it, if the Lord will allow me sufficient strength, I would like to be here to serve during those perilous times.

ARE YOU READY TO SUFFER?

We in the West have experienced little serious persecution for our faith in recent years. That is not the case in much of the world. Daily there are reports of cruelty and martyrdom. In India a seasoned missionary and his two sons were trapped in their car and burned to death by Hindu extremists protesting the proclamation of the gospel of Jesus.

The Christian population in the Sudan has been almost annihilated by rebel forces determined to eradicate the Christian faith.[1] Uganda is still recovering from the death toll exacted during Idi Amin's reign of terror.[2] A brother in northern Iraq was put to death by family members who were "protecting" the family's honor. At the same time there are tens of thousands of new believers because of the faithfulness of those who have risked their lives to spread the good news of the Savior.

As the time of Messiah's return draws near, the warfare will only escalate. Evil and righteousness are maturing together until the harvest, just as Jesus told His listeners in explaining one of the parables (see Matt. 13:30). John sees that harvest in a vision: angels released to gather the righteous into their reward; the wicked thrown into the winepress of the Lord's wrath (see Rev. 14:14-20).

Believers may go through great tribulation, but they will never experience God's wrath. We have been saved from "the coming wrath" through the blood of the Messiah that has been applied, by faith, to the doorposts of our hearts (see Rom. 5:9; 1 Thess. 5:9).

In times of great persecution, many die for their faith. For others, the Lord stays the hand of torturers and executioners.

While in prayer, a sister imprisoned in China felt the shackles drop from her wrists—not unlike Peter's prison experience. Two men on bicycles escaped the secret police, who were pursuing them in a patrol car—the cyclists could be seen but not caught—reminiscent of Pharaoh's thwarted pursuit of Israel at the sea.[3] During the days of Communism, a brother in Ethiopia was beaten mercilessly for preaching the gospel and walked away the following day completely healed—like Paul in an earlier century. Twice that same brother was scheduled for execution by electrocution. Both times a mysterious power failure kept him alive. The frustrated executioners finally released him.[4]

Visible angel warriors and other heavenly messengers are not uncommon in days of great stress. God is carefully watching over His flock to deliver some *from* persecution, while others are being given strength *in* persecution.

The assaults against believers come through human hands, but the plans all have their origin in hell. The Holy Spirit wants us to learn to trust the Lord to care for us, just as he watched over Israel in Goshen, over Daniel in the lions' den, over the early apostles in years of imprisonment, exile or even death. He wants us to have the tenacity of Daniel's friends, who said before being thrown into the blazing furnace, "The God we serve is able to save us. . . . But even if he does not, we want you to know, O king, that we will not serve your gods" (Dan. 3:17,18).

SOMETIME IN THE FUTURE THE WHOLE WORLD WILL TAKE A STAND AGAINST ISRAEL. THEN OUR EARTHLY NATIONALITY WILL NO LONGER BE IMPORTANT. ALL THAT WILL MATTER IS THAT WE ARE BORN-AGAIN-INTO-THE-KINGDOM FELLOW CITIZENS WITH ISRAEL.

Yes, sometime in the future the whole world will take a stand against Israel. All the nations will gather against Jerusalem and bow to a godless ruler. When that day comes, we believers must be ready to come alongside God's covenant people. At that point, our earthly nationality—whether American, Asian, African, Middle Eastern or another—will no longer be important. All that will matter is that we are born-again-into-the-kingdom fellow citizens with Israel.

During the closing days of our stay in "Egypt," our focus is steady. We must rescue others; we must stay in the house with the Lamb's blood on the door; and we must be ready to go at a moment's notice. We want to be sure our spiritual cloaks are tucked into our belts, our sandals are on our feet, our staff is in hand, and we are ready to depart (see Exod. 12:11). When the call comes, the exodus will be abrupt. "In its time I will do this swiftly,"

Isaiah quotes the Lord (Isa. 60:22). "In a flash, in the twinkling of an eye," Paul comments (1 Cor. 15:52).

Centuries of anticipation will give way to a single "suddenly" (Mal. 3:1). Clouds will part, the earth will shake and angel choirs and the redeemed of Adam's children will welcome the returning Messiah. His reign of peace will extend for a thousand years, according to John, before the war to end all wars and the final defeat of mankind's arch enemy (see Rev. 20:7-11).

Only then will the Garden of Eden be restored and heaven and earth joined as God and man—Redeemer and redeemed—dwell together in eternal bliss.

Notes

1. This account was taken from the personal testimony of Sudanese now living in our city.
2. I have traveled to Uganda, held seminars for young preachers who have spoken of these atrocities and have lived in communities with people who were acquainted with these happenings in Uganda during the Idi Amin reign.
3. These incidents are recorded by a Chinese brother who bicycled for six months through China to collect the stories of the Chinese revival. (Danyon, *Lilies Among Thorns* [Kent, England: Sovereign World, Ltd.; distributed in U.S. by Gospel Light, 1991]).
4. Tadesa (an Ethiopian brother), interview by author (April 1999).

BLESSED TO BE A BLESSING

I will bless those who bless you, and whoever curses you I will curse.

GENESIS 12:3

While visiting in Ethiopia in April 1999, we became well acquainted with a man who had served in the royal house of Haile Selassie I, the last emperor of Ethiopia. Haile Selassie, believed by many to have been the 225th descendant of Menelik, the son of King Solomon and the Queen of Sheba, was emperor of Ethiopia from 1930 until 1974. Here is what he told us.

In the early '70s, under pressure from some of the surrounding Arab nations, Selassie broke diplomatic relations with Israel. When his daughter heard the news, she went to her father to warn him of the consequences of his actions. Referring to the Genesis 12:3 blessing on the house of Abraham, she implored him, "My father, my king, you will bring disaster upon our family and upon our people!"

Not many months later, on September 12, 1974, Lt. Colonel Mengistu Haile Miriam, one of Africa's fiercest dictators, seized the reins of power in Ethiopia. Soon afterward Haile Selassie was dead, killed by the man who had engineered his downfall. This event was followed by almost two decades of bloodshed.

Haile Selassie's daughter was right. Whoever touches Israel touches "the apple of [God's] eye" (Zech. 2:8).

Egypt discovered that truth very early in Israel's history. Assyria and Babylon, after being used of God to punish Israel for her disobedience, nevertheless sank into oblivion as world powers soon after their years of cruel tyranny. Spain's navy ruled the seas—until that country killed or expelled her Jewish population. There was a time when the sun never set on the British Empire; that was before Great Britain reneged on the Balfour Declaration. Germany was split in two following the Holocaust, and time has not yet written the final chapter of that story. The Communist governments of Eastern Europe crumbled after years of pogroms and persecution against God's favored son.

The United States has walked in enormous blessing and prosperity through the years as millions of Jewish people have found refuge on our shores. This will no longer be true when she turns her back on God's reestablished government in the Land.

Some prophetic voices are saying that our president has already brought judgment upon our nation by insisting on the very thing the prophet Joel cautioned against—dividing up the land of Israel (see Joel 3:1,2).

Zechariah speaks of a time when all the nations of the world will wage war against this one small country (see Zech. 14:2). Not long ago the United Nations Security Council came close to a foreshadowing of that ominous lineup of nations. The vote taken to censure Israel for building in the "settlements"—biblical Judea and Samaria, the heart of the *Promised* Land—was 17 votes for, 3 against. Only the United States and Micronesia voted with Israel. Dangerous politics.[1]

HOW TO LOVE THE JEWISH PEOPLE

"What has all this to do with me?" you may ask. "I was not a Crusader who burned Jewish synagogues. None of my relatives (as far as I know) were Nazis who sent Jews to the gas chambers. I don't hate Jews."

Though we may not be personally responsible for the indignities suffered by our Jewish brothers and sisters through the years, there are steps we can take to reverse the injustices and actively bless the Jewish people.

**Ask the Lord to cleanse our hearts of
every vestige of anti-Semitism.**
This includes ethnic jokes, gossip and insinuation. A "funny" story or cynical remark will only encourage more discrimination against this persecuted family.

Hatred for the Jews may be buried deeply in our souls, amid the debris of generations of prejudice. We may not even be aware of its presence until we find ourselves joining in the derision.

If God is not finished with Israel, if Israel is destined to accept her Messiah and usher in a future reign of Jesus, if the Church is an heir together with Israel rather than an heir in place of Israel—as I have affirmed throughout this book—and if we have believed to the contrary, then we must repent of having appropriated Jewish Scriptures and Israel's promises for our own without having honored the very people to whom they were originally granted and without including them as part of the Bride of Messiah.

Let the winds of the Holy Spirit blow your heart clean. Reach back in time and listen to God's heart for this priestly nation. Understand why world hatred has been launched against them and allow God's love to rise up to bless them.

Once our own hearts are clean, we can become intercessors—those who stand in the gap, carrying the sins of others in confessional prayer and repentance. Like Daniel, we agonize: "O LORD, we and our kings, our princes and our fathers are covered with shame because we have sinned against you" (Dan. 9:8).

Become aware that the world's news media is prejudiced against God's work and God's people.
Only those who are God-followers can properly assess history, politics and government. Everything in human history, every current event, is moving forward in His timing. We, therefore, will listen to news with greater discernment, always asking ourselves such questions as, "What is the real story behind this

report? What is the Lord doing? How am I to be praying here? Is He expecting me to respond?"

Seek ways to affirm Jewish people, to love them and bless them—whether or not they ever accept Jesus as Messiah.
Jesus spoke of two commandments upon which hang all the Law and the Prophets—loving God and loving each other (see Matt. 22:34-40). Love is active, not passive. We do not love those we ignore, as Jesus so convincingly taught us in the parable of the Good Samaritan.

Just because we have not participated in the Crusades or pogroms of past years does not excuse our passive disinterest in the recurring rise of anti-Semitism throughout the world. If we are not actively righteous, we become passively wicked.

IF THERE WERE NEVER TO BE ANOTHER JEWISH PERSON IN HISTORY WHO BELIEVES IN JESUS AS MESSIAH, WE MUST STILL BE COMMITTED TO THEM AS FRIENDS, BROTHERS, PROTECTORS.

A friend of mine was in Sacramento last year when three of the city's five synagogues were desecrated in one night of cowardly tyranny. Millions of dollars worth of damage was left behind by demonized arsonists. My friend suggested that Christians unite to rebuild the vandalized synagogues. "Oh, and let's save the tracts and the evangelism for another time," he said. "This is a time for blessing with actions."

Paul spoke of living in such a way that makes His people jealous (see Rom. 11:11). That will never happen if all we do is hand out tracts and get into arguments and debates.

Our commitment to Jewish people must never be tied to their acceptance of Yeshua as Messiah. We have been down that road before and it has produced no fruit. If there were never to be another Jewish person in history who believes in Jesus as Messiah, we must still be committed to them as friends, brothers, protectors. Any other action is incongruous with a heart of love.

Prepare for future crises.
On Christmas morning 1999, a group of famous Israelis were being interviewed on national television in Israel about their impressions of Yeshua. Professor Ravitsky, a well-known orthodox scholar, said he realized that had Yeshua been alive in Germany during World War II, He would have been taken to the gas chambers.[2]

Would you have risked your life to save His? Would I? What will I do the next time? These are the kinds of questions we Christians must ask ourselves as we prepare for the future.

Some of my friends are actually building shelters—secret hideaways—to house Jewish people in the coming persecution. Christians in Finland and the rest of Scandinavia have stored food and clothing, bought vehicles for transportation and made other preparations for the next great exodus of Israel's children coming from Russia and the Eastern bloc nations. They want to be the Oskar Schindlers and the Corrie ten Booms, the "righteous Gentiles"—as the Jewish people call them—of our generation.

**Encourage and assist Jewish people to return
to their ancestral inheritance.**

If Ezekiel's word about "not leaving any behind" (Ezek. 39:28) is
to be taken literally—and remember, this is our assumption
unless Scripture clearly indicates otherwise—then we need also
to do our best to make sure they make aliyah to Israel.

In 1973, Steve Lightle gave up his business and began to
travel throughout Europe and Russia, speaking prophetically
about the imminent release of the Russian Jewish population. In
1983 he wrote *Exodus II* to encourage continued readiness.[3] Tom
Hess established the "Jerusalem House of Prayer for All Nations"
and then published his book *Let My People Go* to describe a partnership with God in the prophetic fulfillment that was beginning to take place.[4]

Hess writes,

> Many Jewish people have believed that Israel's security is
> in the military and financial support coming from
> America. The Jewish people need to be warned that while
> the support of America has in many ways been a blessing
> in the past, the future support of Israel will increasingly
> come from God Himself and, hopefully, from her loyal
> Christian Zionist friends around the world.[5]
>
> It is time for the Jewish people in America to set an
> example for the Russian Jews. It is time to break from the
> god of materialism in America and to take whatever wealth
> they have in America back to Israel as they did from Egypt
> and Babylon centuries ago! . . . It is time for the Jews to
> escape the Daughter of Babylon before it is too late.[6]
>
> Precious Jewish people, make Aliyah very soon. Don't
> wait until you have to go. Win the struggle and escape to

Israel today. Come singing and dancing with joy and gladness in Zion, preparing the way for the soon coming of your Messiah and King![7]

Gustav Scheller devoted the last years of his life to the Ebenezer Emergency Fund through which tens of thousands of Jewish people from Eastern Europe were aided in immigrating to Israel. That story is told in *Operation Exodus*. David and Emma Rudolph have established Gateways Beyond to help not only the Eastern Europeans, but also Ethiopian Jews, many of whom are trapped between the two lands. Ethiopians discriminate against them because they are Jews; Israel will not accept many of them because they do not have the proper papers to prove their identity.[8]

Bless the Jewish people financially.

We have already seen how Paul, the Jewish apostle to the Gentiles, incorporated the Jew-Gentile issue into his Roman letter. In the closing verses of this epistle, he makes it clear that "if the Gentiles have shared in the Jews' spiritual blessings, *they owe it to the Jews to share with them their material blessings*" (Rom. 15:27, italics added).

Of course, we know Isaiah predicted that "the wealth on the seas will be brought" (Isa. 60:5), that their gates will remain open "so that men may bring you the wealth of the nations" (v. 11). Millions of Jewish dollars have poured into the reestablishing of the nation since that first Zionist conference in 1897.

A fascinating—even miraculous—story of the days preceding the 1948 War of Independence involves Golda Meir, late prime minister of Israel from 1969 to 1974. Morale in Israel was at its lowest ebb. There was no money for tanks, artillery or aircraft for the war that was sure to come the moment Israel announced its statehood in May of that year. Golda Meir insisted that David ben Gurion should remain at the helm while she, Golda, traveled to the United States to gather funds. There was little hope for the success of this unpretentious, straight-talking carpenter's daughter.

Golda left Israel with no baggage, wearing only a thin spring dress and clutching her almost-empty handbag. She landed in New York City with $10 in her purse and no scheduled speaking appointments. When she returned to Israel only a few days later, the American Jewish community had committed $50 million with which to equip the small Israeli army.[9]

Since that time, the Gentile community too—especially Christians who have been reading prophecy—have come to Israel's aid. After Israel took Jerusalem in the Six Day War of 1967, the United States and other nations refused to move their embassies to the new capital. The "International Christian Embassy Jerusalem" (ICEJ) was formed to assure Israel that thousands of Christians throughout the world disagreed with the decision of their governments. Millions of dollars of support have been funneled to Israel through the efforts of this and similar organizations.

As we grow in understanding, we will also be sure that in our "doing good," we give "especially to those who belong to the family of believers" (Gal. 6:10). Large sums of money are sometimes given by zealous Israel-loving Christians to Jewish organizations that persecute the messianic believers in the Land. Paul's emphasis was always on believers, and he was especially careful to remember the poor (see Rom. 15:26; Gal. 2:10).

As more and more Christians understand Paul's admonition—that we owe it to the Jewish people to bless them financially—we can expect individual Christians and churches, denominational and independent mission agencies to prioritize the financial needs of Israel and the Jewish people, especially the messianic community.

An established messianic ministry recently received a multimillion-dollar gift with which they have been able to purchase a significant historical building to be used as a ministry center in downtown Tel Aviv. The messianic congregation north of Haifa, whose synagogue was firebombed by those who did not like their message, has now been able to purchase a ministry center three times the size of the one that was burned. The arsonists were used of God to alert Christians to the need for a larger and more secure facility! More resources flowed into the same synagogue just recently, following the vandalism in which tires were slashed while a worship service was in session.

It is imperative that we become wise in the distribution of funds. Ask the Lord to open your eyes. Watch where the fruit is being produced rather than becoming carried away by someone who is a great motivator but who may have little to show for years of fund-raising. Attaching the names Israel and Jerusalem to a letterhead can sometimes, perhaps unintentionally, produce sympathy for a ministry that has little connection with the real laborers in the field. Instead, get to know the restored remnant, the actual Jewish believers living in the Land, who are giving themselves to the miraculous latter-day restoration of messianic faith where it all began.

Establish prayer support groups to share in the ministry of those who are on the front lines of the battles.
In Nashville, as in many cities of the world, we have established a prayer shield for Israel and the Jewish people, with links to sev-

eral key ministries both in the Land and in the Diaspora. We welcome messianic Jewish leaders to the city and become prayer partners with them. Their needs become our needs; their joys, our joys; their sorrows, our sorrows. We are often in daily contact through e-mail and can participate with them more effectively, bearing one another's burdens (see Gal. 6:2). We are workers together with God as Paul told the Ephesians (see 2:10), participating in what He initiates.

I have been to Israel several times. The first time—in 1967, shortly before the Six Day War—I had no knowledge of prophecy or of God's purposes for Israel. I only wanted to walk where Jesus walked.

Today when I visit, I go for the purpose of blessing the people of the Land. I encourage every traveler to tithe the cost of the ticket to one of the ministries inside Israel. Each person is also requested to carry two suitcases: one for his or her clothes; the other for restocking the storehouses for Israel's poor.

I further encourage all my brothers and sisters not to leave the Land before becoming acquainted with some of those who are investing their lives in seeing that their own people come to know Israel's Messiah. I am eager for other Christians to see the passion blazing in Asher Intrater's eyes when he speaks of the Lord. To behold the joy on Eitan Shishkoff's face when he welcomes new believers into the family. To watch the love flowing through David and Michaela Lazarus as they wrap their arms around former Russian youth who have now met the Man. To worship in Avner and Rachel Boskey's living room as this anointed couple brings forth their prophetic Hebrew songs. To hear the articulate Reuven Doron with that disarming Israeli accent as he describes God's future plans for His people.

The Lord may give you other ways to bless and to love Jewish people. Jesus told Nicodemus that being born again is by the wind/breath of the Spirit (see John 3:8). We lift our sails to discern the wind and feel the breath of God.

Today the Spirit is blowing Israel back to her Land and breathing new life into Jewish hearts as they open to the good news of their Messiah who has come and will soon return. At the same time, He is sweeping like a tempest across the nations, stirring up the grandest revival of faith in the one true God and his Redeemer-Son that Abraham's children have ever known.

If you are a believer, that same Holy Spirit lives in your heart. Listen to Him and follow where He leads.

Today a new thing is happening among many Christians throughout the world. We see ourselves as Ruth—the non-Jew who has come to faith in Israel's Redeemer. We have come from the famine. We have found bread in the house of our Kinsman-Redeemer Boaz (Jesus).

We are now beginning to go through the house to look for Moabite ways that need to be eliminated in order to restore the furnishings of Israel. We are committing ourselves anew not only to Jesus, Boaz and Ruth's promised Son, but to His relatives. We are welcoming again the customs of the family into which we have been adopted.

We have watched in the past as this family of ours has been persecuted and maligned. We grieve with our brothers and sisters over their pain, which was often inflicted at the hands of our own ancestors in the faith.

We are saying to our Jewish family: "Your people shall be my people, and your God, my God" (Ruth 1:16, *NKJV*). A growing number of us are stirred in our spirits. We are ready to make a bold declaration—one that might be tested at any moment. We are ready to say with Ruth (see v. 17): I am ready to die with you and be buried with you. May the Lord deal with me, be it ever so severely, if anything but death separates you and me.

Notes

1. This UN resolution, first passed in 1996 and reaffirmed in 1999, states that "Israeli settlements in the Palestinian territory, including Jerusalem, and in the occupied Golan are illegal and an obstacle to peace and economic and social development" and "calls upon Israel to accept the *de jure* applicability of the Geneva Convention . . . to the occupied territory," and "demands complete cessation of all illegal Israeli settlements." In both 1996 and 1999, only Israel, the United States and Micronesia voted against the resolution. These statistics are posted on the United Nations website.
2. A Channel 1 interview broadcast in Hebrew on December 25, 1999, on the program "Popolitika," in which three Israelis spoke of their impressions of Yeshua. In addition to Professor Ravitsky, a leader in Israeli television stated that he hated Jesus and blamed Him for the murder of his parents—until he had a chance to read the New Testament. It was then he realized that he had to separate the history between Judaism and Christianity from the person of Yeshua. He encouraged all Israelis to read the New Testament. The head of all Israeli security forces suggested that the teachings of Yeshua are more appropriate for Israelis today than the teachings of the rabbis.
3. For many stories of preparation for the coming exodus, see Steve Lightle, *Exodus II: Let My People Go, Section II* (Kingwood, TX: Hunter Books, 1983).
4. Tom Hess, *Let My People Go: The Struggle of the Jewish People to Return to Israel*, 5th ed. (Charlotte, NC: MorningStar Publications, 1997), n.p.
5. Ibid., p. 30.
6. Ibid., pp. 70, 75.
7. Ibid., p. 109.
8. See Appendix C for further information about the Ebenezer Emergency Fund and Gateways Beyond ministries.

9. Larry Collins and Dominique Lapierre, *O Jerusalem! Day by Day and Minute by Minute: The Historic Struggle for Jerusalem and the Birth of Israel* (New York: Simon and Schuster, 1972), pp. 162-166.

TOWARD JERUSALEM COUNCIL II

Jerusalem Council II is a vision to repair and heal the breach between Jewish and Gentile believers in Yeshua, dating from the first centuries of the Church, and to do so primarily through humility, prayer and repentance.

Who?

Prayer representatives of the Gentile Christian community and the Messianic Jewish community. These representatives should be builder-leaders in various communities, who practice a life of prayer.

What?

Jerusalem Council II is based on these Scriptures:

Acts 15—The Council
Acts 21:17-26—The Messianic Jewish View
Romans 11:29—The Irrevocable Call to Israel
2 Corinthians 5:18,19—Reconciliation
Ephesians 2:11-16—One New Man

Toward Jerusalem Council II is a meeting of Gentile Christian and Messianic Jewish leaders to foster these goals to:

1. Recognize the schism between Jewish and Gentile brethren created by the early Church, especially culminating in the decrees of the Nicene Council II. Repair and heal this breach through humility, repentance, prayer and intercessory representation on the part of both Gentile Christians and messianic Jews, including prayer for the recanting and rescinding of the anti-messianic Jewish decrees which declared that messianic Jewish communities had no right to exist. These decrees have hovered over the Body of Messiah for at least 16 centuries.

2. Pray to be reconciled in heart and to call for all true believers to affirm the reality of our reconciliation as one new man. Recognize that true reconciliation is not the result of diluting one's identity, but is the miracle of breaking down the wall of partition through the blood of the Messiah so that the two identifiable groups can become one new man (Eph. 2).

3. Understand the Jewish roots of Christianity. The Bible is essentially a Jewish book written primarily by Jews, and the Jewish people were entrusted with the oracles of God with which the world is to be blessed. Jesus was Jewish; all of His first disciples and apostles were Jews; and the first congregation of believers were all Jewish. Jews and Gentiles alike who turn their hearts toward God are turning toward the Lord God of Israel "who was, and is, and is to come" (Rev. 4:8)–"the same yesterday, today, and forever" (Heb. 13:8). Our faith has its roots in the Jewish people. Anti-Semitism is a most heinous sin to be repudiated by all Christian people.

4. Recognize the sacrificial, loving effort of true believers from among the Gentiles to share the Good News of the Messiah with the Jewish people. We, as messianic Jews, are called on to repent of sinful attitudes and actions, of pride, arrogance, fear and isolation toward the rest of the Body of the Messiah. We must pray for the integrity, stability, restoration and evangelistic progress of the Church. We also are called to repudiate decisions taken since the days of the apostles to direct the Jewish community away from faith in the Messiah, Yeshua.

5. Encourage Gentile Christians as individual believers and as churches to recognize and to grieve over the Church's sins against Jewish believers in Jesus (1) for all forms of "replacement" teaching that treated the first covenant as obsolete (due to Jewish rejection of Jesus as Messiah) and saw the (Gentile) Church as replacing Israel and inheriting Israel's promises, thus ignoring the scriptural promise of Romans 11:29 that says "God's gifts and his call are irrevocable"; (2) for the rejection and suppression of any Jewish expression of faith in Yeshua, and for all requirements that Jews believing in Yeshua should repudiate their Jewish identity and all their Jewish practices; (3) for the

seeds of Church division that were sown by the repudiation of the community of Jewish believers in Yeshua (Jesus) and its denial of the "one new man" of Ephesians 2.

6. Understand and appreciate the validity of the Messianic Jewish community:

A. That God is once again doing a great work among our Jewish brethren for the salvation and redemption of Israel.

B. That Jews who turn to the Messiah are free and encouraged to remain distinctly Jewish in accord with the apostolic Jewish life pattern—including the circumcision of their sons as well as walking according to the pattern of Jewish life as is rightly applicable in the New Covenant.

C. Our Gentile brethren are called upon to affirm and pray for the doctrinal and moral integrity, stability and the evangelistic progress of the messianic Jewish community. Gentile brethren are called to take up the imperative of intercession and support for the salvation of Israel.

7. Pray for and call for the Church to affirm a declaration similar to that of Acts 15, whereby Jews who follow Jesus would be affirmed in their continued Jewish life and calling within the context of scriptural norms.

For more information on the Toward Jerusalem Council II, contact one of our co-chairs:

Marty Waldman
Baruch HaShem Congregation
6304 Belt Line Road
Dallas, TX 75240

John Dawson
International Reconciliation Council
P.O. Box 278
Ventura, CA 93006

APPENDIX B

RECOMMENDED READING

Bennett, Ramon. *When Day and Night Cease: A Prophetic Study of World Events and How Prophecy Concerning Israel Affects the Nations, the Church and You.* Jerusalem: Arm of Salvation Press, 1992.

Brown, Michael L. *Our Hands Are Stained with Blood: The Tragic Story of the "Church" and the Jewish People.* Shippensburg, PA: Destiny Image Publishers, 1992.

Cantor, Ron. *I Am Not Ashamed.* Gaithersburg, MD: Tikkun International, 1999.

Chernoff, Yohanna. *Born a Jew . . . Die a Jew: The Story of Martin Chernoff, a Pioneer in Messianic Judaism.* Hagerstown, MD: EBED Publications, 1996.

Collins, Larry and Dominique Lapierre, *O Jerusalem! Day by Day and Minute by Minute: The Historic Struggle for Jerusalem and the Birth of Israel.* NY: Simon and Schuster, 1972.

Damkani, Jacob. *Why Me?* New Kensington, PA: Whitaker House, 1997.

DolAn, David. *Israel at the Crossroads, Fifty Years and Counting.* Grand Rapids, MI: Fleming H. Revell, 1998.

Doron, Reuven. *One New Man.* Cedar Rapids, IA: Embrace Israel, 1996.

Flynn, Leslie B. *What the Church Owes the Jew.* Carlsbad, CA: Magnus Press, 1998.

Frydland, Rachmiel. *What the Rabbis Know About the Messiah, A Study of Genealogy and Prophecy.* Cincinnati, OH: Messianic Publishing Company, 1991.

Hess, Tom. *Let My People Go: The Struggle of the Jewish People to Return to Israel,* 5th ed. Charlotte, NC: MorningStar Publications, 1997.

_____. *The Watchmen: Being Prepared and Preparing the Way for Messiah.* Washington, DC: Progressive Vision International, 1998.

Hocken, Peter. *The Glory and the Shame: Reflections on the 20th Century Outpouring of the Holy Spirit.* Guildford, England: Eagle, 1994.

Juster, Dan. *The Irrevocable Calling.* Gaithersburg, MD: Tikkun Ministries, 1996.

_____. *Jewish Roots.* Shippensburg PA: Destiny Image Publishers, 1995.

_____. *One People, Many Tribes: A Primer on Church History from a Messianic Jewish Perspective.* Clarence, NY: Kairos Publishers, 1999.

_____. *Revelation: The Passover Key.* Shippensburg PA: Destiny Image Publishers, 1991.

Juster, Dan and Keith Intrader. *Israel, the Church and the Last Days.* Shippensburg, PA: Destiny Image Publishers, 1990.

Kjaer-Hansen, Kai. *Joseph Rabinowitz and the Messianic Movement: The Herzl of Jewish Christianity.* Grand Rapids, MI: Wm. B. Eerdmans, 1995.

Kjaer-Hansen, Kai, and Bodil F. Skjott, *Facts and Myths About the Messianic Congregations in Israel.* Jerusalem: United Christian Council in Israel in cooperation with the Caspari Center for Biblical and Jewish Studies, 1999.

Levine, David. *In That Day: How Jesus Is Revealing Himself to the Jewish People in These Last Days.* Lake Mary, FL: Creation House, Strang Communications, 1998.

Lightle, Steve. *Exodus II: Let My People Go.* Kingwood, TX: Hunter Books, 1983.

Murray, Iain H. *The Puritan Hope: Revival and the Interpretation of Prophecy.* Carlisle, PA: The Banner of Truth Trust, 1998.

Otis, George, Jr. *The Last of the Giants.* Tarrytown, NY: Chosen Books, Fleming H. Revell, 1991.

Portnov, Dr. Anna, comp. *Awakening: An Anthology of Articles, Essays, Biographies, and Quotations About Jews and Yeshua (Jesus).* Baltimore, MD: Lederer Publications, 1992.

Pritz, Ray A. *Nazarene Jewish Christianity: From the End of the New Testament Period Until Its Disappearance in the Fourth Century.* 1988. Reprint, Jerusalem: The Magnus Press, Hebrew University, 1992.

Rosen, Ruth. *Jewish Doctors Meet the Great Physician.* San Francisco: Purple Pomegranate Productions, 1998.

_____. *Testimonies of Jews Who Believe in Jesus.* San Francisco: Purple Pomegranate Productions, 1992.

Roth, Sid. *There Must Be Something More: The Spiritual Rebirth of a Jew.* Brunswick, GA: MV Press, 1994.

_____. *They Thought for Themselves.* Brunswick, GA: MV Press, 1996.

Scheller, Gustav, *Operation Exodus: Prophecy Being Fulfilled.* Kent, England: Sovereign World Limited, 1998.

Schiffman, Michael. *Return of the Remnant: The Rebirth of Messianic Judaism.* Baltimore, MD: Lederer Messianic Publishers, 1992.

Stern, David H. *Messianic Jewish Manifesto.* Clarksville, MD: Jewish New Testament Publications, 1988.

_____. *Complete Jewish Bible: An English Version of the Tanakh (Old Testament) and B'rit Hadashah (New Testament).* Clarksville, MD: Jewish New Testament Publications, 1998.

_____. *Restoring the Jewishness of the Gospel.* Jerusalem: Jewish New Testament Publications, 1988.

Telchin, Stan. *Betrayed.* Old Tappan, NJ: Chosen Books, Fleming H. Revell, 1981.

Teplinsky, Sandra. *Out of the Darkness: The Untold Story of Jewish Revival in the Former Soviet Union.* Jacksonville Beach, FL: Hear O Israel Publishing, 1998.

Urbach, Eliezer. *Out of the Fury: The Incredible Odyssey of Eliezer Urbach.* Charlotte, NC: Chosen People Ministries, 1987.

Wilson, Marvin R. *Our Father Abraham: Jewish Roots of the Christian Faith.* 1989. Reprint, Grand Rapids, MI: William B. Eerdmans, 1994.

MESSIANIC JEWISH MOVEMENTS AND CONGREGATIONS

For further information on the messianic Jewish movement and congregations, you may contact:

Tikkun (Restoration)
P. O. Box 2997
Gaithersburg, MD 20886

Hear O Israel Ministries
P.O. Box 30990
Phoenix, AZ 85046-0990

Messianic Jewish Alliance of America (MJAA)
P. O. Box 274
Springfield, PA 19064

Union of Messianic Jewish Congregations (UMJC)
P. O. Box 11113
Burke, VA 22009-1113

For ministries in Israel and the Diaspora mentioned in this book, you may contact:

Asher Intrater
P. O. Box 485
Beit Shemesh
ISRAEL
Fax: (011-972-671-0279)
www.revive-israel.org

Eitan Shishkoff
Tents of Mercy (*Ohalei Rachamim*)
P. O. Box 1018
Kiryat Yam 29109
ISRAEL
Tel: 972-4-877-7921
E-mail: ohalei@netvision.net.il

Gateways Beyond
P. O. Box 1131
Colonial Heights, VA 23834
Tel./Fax: (804) 526-6296
E-mail: gatewaysbeyond@juno.com

Gateways Beyond, Cyprus
P. O. Box 54516, CY 3733
Limassol, Cyprus
Tel: (357) 543-4560
Fax: (357) 543-2090
E-mail: gatewaysbeyond@cylink.com.cy

Ebenezer Emergency Fund
P. O. Box 271653
Fort Collins, CO 80527

www.tikkunministries.org

For a Jewish Ministry Training program or ways to
bless and serve the Jewish people, contact the YWAM
Jewish World Office at www.YWAMVA.org or call
(804) 236-8898.

You may contact me personally at:

The Caleb Company
Don Finto
68 Music Square East
Nashville, TN 37203
www.calebcompany.com

APPENDIX D

STATEMENT OF REPENTANCE

TO THE JEWISH PEOPLE IN AMERICA AND THE NATIONS OF THE WORLD*

Dear Respected Friends in the Jewish Community who share in our common faith in the G-d of Abraham, Isaac, and Jacob,

Something is happening in our generation that we deem to be motivated by the Almighty. People of different ethnic backgrounds and national origins are acknowledging the sins of past generations against each other in a desire for reconciliation and peace. The sons and daughters of former slave traders are taking upon themselves the sins of their forebears and confessing these sins to the sons and daughters of former slaves. You may be aware that a "Reconciliation Walk" was recently taken between Europe and Jerusalem by a group of Christians who were confessing the sins and devastations of the Crusaders.

We know that the Jewish people throughout the centuries have borne the greatest discrimination, the worst persecution, and the most barbaric atrocities of all. We, too, have read the histories. We are aware that much of this has been done by Christians or by those who called themselves Christians, sometimes while calling upon the name of Christ. This is a grotesque misrepresentation of the One who is called the Prince of Peace and who called us to love and worship our Heavenly Father, and to love our neighbor as ourselves. Though the Scriptures we call the New Testament have exhorted us to love, respect and exercise mercy towards you, the ancient people of G-d, and G-d's chosen people to this day, we and our forefathers in the Christian faith have rebelled against that command and have acted out of fear, prejudice, hatred and jealousy. Those who have not so acted have acquiesced by their silence during the times of crusades, pogroms, and finally in the terrifying holocaust.

Nor are we Christian believers in the United States without our own share in this guilt. Not only are many of us descended from the perpetrators of these crimes, but our forefathers stood by without registering complaint when, in the years of the reign of horror in Europe, Jewish refugees were turned away from our shores. Our forefathers turned their eyes away from the death plight of the European Jewish community. Even in recent years, some in the Christian community have often stood in apathy as synagogues have been torched, cemeteries desecrated, and Jewish homes and businesses vandalized.

We grieve over these crimes against you, our Jewish brothers and sisters, and in the spirit of Daniel, who confessed the sins of former generations, we confess these horrors as sins and renounce them. We understand from our reading of the Prophet Zechariah that a time will yet come when the whole world turns against Israel. Should such a thing come to pass, many of us want to be numbered with those few Gentile Christians through the centuries who have risked their lives to protect you. We commit ourselves to standing with you in the strength of G-d, whatever the cost.

* Used by permission of Generals of Intercession, P.O. Box 49788, Colorado Springs, CO 80949; fax: 719-535-0884; website: www.generals.org.